Born in 1962, Colin Fry received his first message at the age of ten and became a professional medium at seventeen. He has toured internationally and has his own television show, *6ixth Sense*, on Living TV. As one of the elder statesmen of the psychic mediumship world, Colin is more than qualified to use his spiritual knowledge to offer life-changing advice and support to people, providing sensible down-to-earth explanations about the strange world of the paranormal and supernatural.

# Life Before Death

## Colin Fry

**RIDER**

LONDON · SYDNEY · AUCKLAND · JOHANNESBURG

1 3 5 7 9 10 8 6 4 2

Published in 2007 by Rider, an imprint of Ebury Publishing

Ebury Publishing is a division of the Random House Group

The Random House Group Limited Reg. No. 954009
Addresses for companies within the Random House Group can be
found at www.randomhouse.co.uk

A CIP catalogue record for this book is available from the British
Library

The Random House Group Limited makes every effort to ensure
that the papers used in our books are made from trees that have
been legally sourced from well-managed and credibly certified
forests. Our paper procurement policy can be found on
www.randomhouse.co.uk

Printed and bound in Great Britain by Cox and Wyman Ltd,
Reading, Berkshire

ISBN 978-1-8460-4080-1

# Contents

# Contents

## Acknowledgements

We are all the sum of our experiences, but more importantly it is the people we meet in life that enrich and give colour, warmth, and depth to them.

I would like to thank:

John and Geraldine Austin, Pat Cole, Justine Cargill (née Gardner) and Jonathan Cargill for the many years of dedicated commitment they gave to guiding my development.

George Cranley, for being the friend and mentor that everyone needs, but few are ever privileged to find in life.

Eden James, my manager, for being the best friend I could ever want.

Craig and Hilary Goldman, for sharing my vision and bringing my career to a far greater audience than I had ever dreamed of.

Vivienne Foster, my tour organiser – who works magic! – and who puts up with all my moods.

Tim and Tony, my crew, who remind me to smile and stay sane.

Mark, for being a life-long friend, and Chris and Vince for sharing so much of the journey with me and enabling me to fly.

Friends are important to me and I keep them few and close: Darren, I thank you for making me believe in myself when I almost stopped, I will always value our friendship; Andy and Matt, you will always know where you are in my heart.

And Michael Zucker, Claire Baylin and Lena Seeman for organising my thoughts, ideas and words in the preparation of this book.

Arthur and Margaret Fry – my parents who have always been there and always believed in me.

To all the people I have named in these acknowledgements: you have all played your part and taught me things that have made this book possible.

And to those who have hurt me – what doesn't kill you makes you stronger – thank you.

Love and light,

Colin Fry

I dedicate this book to two people:
Michael Patrick Cotton (in Spirit) – my friend,
my guardian, my angel, my brother, you taught me
the value of life

Mikey, my civil partner, who helped me to realise
that you are never too old to love again

# Introduction

*'It is only when we truly know and understand that we have a limited time on earth – and we have no way of knowing when that time is up – that we will begin to live each day to the fullest as if it was the only one we had.'*

**DR ELISABETH KÜBLER-ROSS**

I don't think that anything can be as emotionally challenging as coming to terms with the death of a child. Over many years as a working medium I have passed on countless messages to grief-stricken parents from children who have passed to the spirit world. A common feeling when a child passes over is that one or both of the parents believe that they cannot continue to live without that child and wish to join them. One such case was Sylvia. Sylvia's eldest child and only son, Stephen had been born with cystic fibrosis and the doctors had predicted that Stephen would not have a long life. Nonetheless, with the dedicated care of his family Stephen had a happy childhood and developed a great passion for music to the extent that he became an accomplished musician, learning both guitar and piano.

Tragically Stephen passed away in his sleep just after his thirteenth birthday and although he had always been a very sick lad the sudden nature of his passing left the whole family devastated. For his mother Sylvia, it was particularly hard. Once the funeral had passed, her initial feelings of sadness began to mix with feelings of anger and resentment that it was 'unfair' her child had been taken from her. This then caused Sylvia to fall into a deep state of despair and depression. She lost all interest in herself and the rest of her family. Life seemed to her to have very little point and in her mind the only thing she could do was join her child in spirit.

The rest of her family were beside themselves with worry. They had no idea how to help her. Her poor husband Ray was attempting to deal with his own terrible sense of loss while accompanying her on visits to the family doctor and bereavement counsellors but nothing seemed to help her past this loss. At the suggestion of a family friend they persuaded Sylvia to see a medium.

As is often the case with people who visit mediums, Sylvia had convinced herself that Stephen would say specific things to her and give certain pieces of evidence if he was able to communicate from the spirit side of life. However, after having visited a great number of mediums she was at the point of giving up in despair as nothing had convinced her that Stephen was able to communicate from the other side of life. It was a chance meeting with a lady at a Spiritualist church in her home town of Newcastle that persuaded Sylvia to contact me.

On the day that Sylvia made her visit to me all I was aware

of was that a lady by the name of Sylvia was coming by train from Newcastle to see me for a reading. As soon as she arrived at my home and was settled in a chair before me, the feeling of her son Stephen's spirit presence became very clear to me and I still think of this sitting as one of the most clear and direct communications I have ever sensed. Many communicators follow a pattern of emphasising evidence of their identity as a prelude to the communication but in Stephen's case he wanted to get straight to the point of his communication.

'Stephen is telling me to tell you that YOU MUST NOT do as you plan when you leave this sitting today. It will NOT bring you closer together and will ruin everything.' At this Sylvia became most agitated.

'I don't know what you're talking about,' she said.

'I think you might, Sylvia. I'm afraid your son is showing me that he's aware you intend to jump in front of a train when you leave me today.'

Upon hearing this Sylvia collapsed into floods of uncontrollable tears and confessed that this was in fact true. 'What else can I do?' she said.

Feeling strongly that Stephen would be able to hold his link with me, I paused the sitting to make Sylvia some strong sweet tea and to give her time to compose herself. What followed was probably one of the most loving and heart-warming communications between a son to his mother I have ever been privileged to pass on.

Stephen made many references to other family members: his sisters and his father, aunts and uncles who had all played such a vital part in his life. He asked me to give as evidence many happy memories he'd had of his life on this side with his family.

'He wants to give you his deepest love and gratitude.'

Sylvia, now in tears, nodded.

Most importantly he went on to explain that he had come to understand that everyone has their time to be on this earth and a time to move on.

'He is saying he was only meant to be here for a short time and that it was a good thing for everybody.'

'How?' said Sylvia, trying not to cry.

'Stephen is telling me that even though his life was affected by his chronic illness, he believes that it is the reason why he had such a deeply loving, supportive family. You all had to pull together to look after him.'

He went on to explain that by taking her own life, Sylvia could not guarantee that in the vastness of an eternal spirit world she would be instantly reunited with him.

'Tell Mum her time will come. It's not now.'

His message was that by interfering with the natural progression of her existence Sylvia might well create a situation where she would not be reunited with him until such point as the intended time of her passing. 'You will leave behind the people who love you. And you just can't do that, Mum. Don't do it.'

One of the roles of a medium is to help people stop thinking of themselves as passive victims of life events and instead start to think of themselves as people who can learn to manage the despair and disappointment of life and move forwards. Life is always worth living, no matter how tough it might be and that was explicit in what Stephen was telling his mother.

If I could divide up the messages I receive they fall broadly into two categories. Firstly a spirit wants to let their loved ones know that they are all right. They often mention the names of fellow family members and friends who passed over to show they are in good company and not alone. Secondly, they often feel the need to pass on advice or encouragement/moral support where needed. The spirits do not describe their living conditions; what concerns them instead is that their loved ones are doing well here on earth as in my opening story. This is what concerns me too: as interesting and satisfying as it is to hear from the other side, it is our responsibility to deal with the here and now.

After most theatre shows I get to stay behind and meet with members of the audience. The one question I receive almost every evening is, 'Do you not find it depressing thinking about death the whole time?' The truth is I rarely think about death, even when I'm communicating with the spirit world. I am thinking about living my life in the most positive way possible and encouraging others to do the same. If we don't, then it's us who are dead to the world, not those who I am in contact with. Stephen's message to his mother was not to become one of those people who are dead to the world.

During one of my own private conversations with Magnus, my spirit guide (a spirit mentor whose relationship with a medium develops as the medium develops his or her own skills), he told me: 'It is a human characteristic to set your sights on horizons. The danger of this is you can be tempted to rush towards them, only to find that when you reach them there is another horizon and what you lost in your haste was the joy, experience and learning of the journey.' Even in the sadness of having loved ones pass before us to that far horizon we have no choice but to take the slow path to join them as we have to accumulate the joys and pleasures of further human life so we can ultimately journey together to even further horizons. We can't see the big picture of existence from our position, but maybe we have to trust that there is a fairness to it all.

Some months after Sylvia came to visit me I received a letter from her thanking me for the experience of the sitting and the evidence from Stephen but mostly because she believed that if the sitting had not taken place in the manner it had, she would have indeed taken her own life and one moment of tragedy in her family's life would have gone on to cause a lifetime of sorrow for so many more.

With this in mind, I thought that rather than only write about what I think might happen in the afterlife, I want to focus this book on how we live our lives before we die and give you examples of what we can learn from readings. Let's face it: no-one wants to die. Yet it is unavoidable. We cannot choose how we die but we can choose how we live. And for me that means living each day to the fullest, without fear or regret. We can make a decision to make the most of every moment in our lives so that we benefit not only ourselves but others. And if we do manage this and don't waste our precious time on this earth then our lives will have purpose and meaning.

When I speak of meaning I am talking about what matters to you, not anybody else. Your life is your own so it's best not to waste it living somebody else's. Each of us has our own gifts. The hairdresser, the writer, the florist, the baker, the counsellor: they all have something they can do to the best of their ability. Whether they do or not depends on their self-discipline and their determination to ignore what others are achieving and concentrate on their own achievements instead. The key is not to covet someone else's gifts but celebrate your own. And remember, the grass is not greener on the other side. Everyone has their problems in life. We seem to live in an age where society presents us with superficialities and encourages us to compete for non-existent and non-meaningful goals. We should be positive about the wonderful potential available to us.

When asked if I think being a medium makes me feel abnormal or extraordinary I reply that I consider myself to be a totally normal person leading a normal life with a normal gift – that some people think is an extraordinary gift. I don't believe that I'm particularly special. I have the same financial worries as anyone else, the same health issues. I have dreams of places I wish to visit, and goals I want to achieve. No-one should put me on a pedestal; I'm a normal guy, who likes a smoke, and a drink just like everyone else. Mediumship just happens to be my gift but we all have gifts. Some people are born with good hands, others with high intelligence, and others with the ability to swerve a football in mid-flight. Some can create music or art and others can put a smile on other people's faces and ease their burdens. I just happened to be born with heightened senses – an ability to tune into different frequencies of communication. As in any profession or vocation I get to meet others with gifts similar to my own, and people with overrated or under-developed abilities. I can have a good day or a bad day like anybody else. My gift is really no more special than yours.

One of the first times I really stopped and thought about what it is I actually do professionally was at the start of my career, when I had to fill in a rather boring life insurance application form. I raced through and ticked my way through the various sections until I came to the one marked 'job description'. Goodness me, I thought, whatever shall I put down here? At that point it all became a bit comical as I paused and asked the broker how best to express on the form that I was a psychic medium and that I primarily communicated with dead people for a living?

There was much 'tut-tutting' and eyebrow-raising as everyone searched for a solution. In the end, after I'd produced various materials showing that I had given demonstrations for charities, Spiritualist churches and newspaper interviews, the rather surprised broker remarked – and he was only half-joking – that I should fill in the form with the words '*life assessor*'. His opinion was that if I couldn't see myself dying in the near future, then an actuary in head office was unlikely to predict anything different! My application was duly accepted.

The truth is, of course, that I can no more predict the future than you can, but I have been communicating with the spirit world since I was ten years old. I truly believe that I was born with the gift of being a psychic medium, although it took many years to learn how to harness this gift, and several more to realise how it should be used to bring comfort and support to those who might need it. In the past few years we've have seen a big increase in the publicity surrounding psychic abilities, especially in the United Kingdom. I have been very fortunate to have been one of those involved as it has allowed me to present my mediumship to ever widening audiences.

I can only speak for myself here and describe how I am able to receive a message from a soul in the spirit world. Sometimes I hear a voice, sometimes I can see a person, but more often than not I sense the spirit of a departed soul. It is almost as if that soul impresses its personality over my thoughts, allowing me to use my five normal senses to express what they are trying to tell me. The spirit will give me evidence of their continued existence by telling me things about the person who sits in front of me that are personal to them. By relating these things I hope to pass on the message that they continue to exist.

The function of a good medium is not just to tune into these messages, but also to try and interpret them in the right way. I have always felt that there are two main types of medium. There are those who are gifted to receive specific accurate information such as street names or exact dates of birth, and others like myself who concentrate on passing on an emotional resonance from a spirit and not just dry facts. Almost all mediums are psychic, but not all psychics are mediums.

This book is not going to prove to you that I or anybody else is a psychic medium. I cannot, nor wish to, 'prove to you' anything. Nor do I wish to change anybody's belief system or religious faith. Ultimately belief is as real as you want it to be. Most people will accept supporting evidence for the things they believe in and reject evidence for things they don't believe in. In short it is often the believer who provides the belief. This book also cannot prove to you that there is an afterlife. I know there is. The messages I have personally experienced from the spirit world have convinced me that there is life after death, that our spirits and personalities continue to exist after our physical bodies die. Of course millions of people across the globe of many faiths already believe this, irrespective of what I claim to see, sense or hear when I practise my mediumship. I can tell you what I believe, but you the reader will have to make up your own mind. That, after all, is what much of living is about.

When I was starting out and unaware of how raw my abilities were, I was privileged to meet the grand dame of British mediumship Ms Doris Stokes. In my arrogance I asked her to advise me on when she thought I'd be ready to take my mediumship to the highest levels. She smiled back at me and said, 'When you're older and have lost your loved ones, when you have suffered the pains of experience and when you grow a few grey hairs then you'll be ready.' Sad to say I have long passed all of her benchmarks, but with her thoughts in mind I wish to assure you that all the episodes in this book actually happened to me, although I have changed names to respect people's privacy. Some stories might seem fantastic, but I assure you they are all true to the best of my knowledge and many of them happened in front of large theatre audiences or in a TV studio.

But this isn't about me. It's about how I can help you. Through stories of my readings as well as my own experiences in life I've tried to give you some ideas and suggestions to motivate you to embrace life to the fullest. It isn't comprehensive by any means but what I hope this book will do for you is help you cut through the confusion of messages that we all deal with in our lives today so that you can clear your own head and work out what and who matters to you. No matter what your faith or beliefs, I sincerely hope this book will help provide some food for thought in your quest for spiritual growth.

Colin Fry

# 1.

# Are you living or existing?

*'There is no cure for birth and death, save to enjoy the interval.'*

**GEORGE SANTAYANA**

How many times have you heard yourself say, 'I wish I'd done that'? It's perfectly normal to have missed opportunities or passed them up in our lives and it's something that all of us have done at various times, since it's not always practical to take advantage of everything. The real problem is when you start making excuses for not doing anything with your life. When you start hearing yourself saying things like, 'I'll get around to it one day. Maybe when I'm not so busy/have some money/lose some weight' that you need to ask yourself the really serious question: 'Am I leading a life or just waiting for one to happen?'

While you're thinking about that, take a moment to consider

this: as humans we are not productive from the moment we are born. In fact it takes us quite a few years to get going and acquire the basic knowledge that we need in order to feed, dress and look after ourselves in general. Then, add in the years we are ill or infirm until we finally get old and need to be looked after again. Ultimately out of, say, the eighty or so years that make up the average lifespan, we don't have that many years where we can actually be properly productive.

I'm sorry if that sounds a bit scary, but I deliberately wanted to give you a wake-up call, a very simple one. I believe that you and I need to make sure we make the most of our time here *in a way that is meaningful both to ourselves and to others*. Humans have a unique ability in that we can choose what we want to do, who we want to be and who we want to share our lives with. Something I'm asked a lot is, 'Do you think we are all part of some grand plan – are we travelling along a pre-destined journey?' My feeling is that we are all on different fixed paths, but along those paths we have the ability to travel as we choose.

## No-one else can choose for you

Being free to choose is one of the most important things about being human. Of course freedom of choice also brings with it the burden and responsibility of making the 'right' choices, whatever they may be. That doesn't mean we can live our lives perfectly, never making mistakes, but it does mean that we need to be able to manage our lives. Nobody else is responsible for our actions except us: that is what living is all about. If we opt out of taking the responsibility and wait for others to rescue us and make it better, we are not really living, we are just existing and that to me is just a criminal waste of our time on this earth.

Because we only get one chance to live our lives in a

physical sense, wouldn't it be useful to have some lessons to help us along the way? I believe this is where our communication with the afterlife can help us. When a spirit chooses to pass on messages, I believe they do so for a reason. The fact that they have made the effort to communicate suggests there may be something we can learn from them. The messages can often be deceptively simple but that doesn't make them any less relevant or compelling.

One evening a few years ago, I was drowning. I had lost control; in fact I was trapped and the water was rising at an alarming rate, wrapping itself around me. The natural warmth of my body had left me, my feet became very cold, and I started to lose feeling in my toes.

The water level continued to climb until it reached my chin and then slowly started to lap beside my mouth. Around me I could hear shouting, but I could not fully understand who was doing it or what was being said. It was very, very dark and gloomy. Not far away I could sense other people but had no idea exactly where they were or if they were still alive. I struggled as the water rose up over my mouth. I had to tilt my head back if I was to have any chance of breathing through my nose and hanging on. Finally when I felt like I was being dragged under, a bright light shone into my eyes. I was suddenly being pulled upwards. My body was aching but I was safe. For a few seconds I was stunned and then I was back on stage again, relieved that the suffocating feeling of wetness in my nostrils had gone …

I have received messages before from those who have drowned, but never in so much detail, and never with such urgency. It was a very vivid and specific memory. It also turned out that there was one man in this particular audience who knew exactly what I was talking about. I later found out his name was Steve. Steve didn't take long to put his hand up.

'I know who it is,' he said. 'It's my father.'

The extraordinary level of detail I had received from Steve's dad was not because he had drowned: it was because he had survived and come through it all. I continued with the thoughts he was asking me to convey.

'He says that it taught him something and he wants you to hear it.'

'What is it?' asked Steve expectantly.

It was actually a very simple message and I wondered if Steve would be disappointed.

'It taught me, son. It taught me to make the most of the time that was left.'

Steve's father continued with his message and went on to talk about his love of motorbike riding and the various and numerous accidents Steve had been in, often questioning his driving skills!

'Remember the pub, son?'

Steve smiled.

'He's showing me a lump of something. It looks very much like burnt wood.'

'No,' said Steve. 'It's carved out of coal. Dad was a coal miner.'

An hour later, after the demonstration was finished I spoke to Steve, who explained his father had been a coal miner in Yorkshire.

'He was trapped for a very long time when the pit caved in. Dad was close to drowning but was rescued at the last minute,' said Steve. 'I remember he was in a lot of shock but one of the first things he asked was, "Where are my friends?"'

'Did he know what might have happened to them?' I rather suspected I knew the answer.

'They drowned,' Steve confirmed sadly.

Following this tragic episode, Steve said, his father felt he could no longer continue doing the same work. He was happy to spend his remaining years with his family.

'He seemed to have a renewed interest in life after that. Even the smallest things excited him. He never took anything for granted.'

Steve's dad had used the accident to take a good look at his life and rearrange his priorities. What had happened to him is something that's pretty common with people who've been through a major trauma. They tend to see life in a fresh, new light and often want others to feel the same way and feel their passion. I think Steve's father felt that his son needed a reminder at this point in his life not to wait for a sign in order to live his life to the fullest. It certainly gave the audience something to think about.

One of the key things about 'living' is the way we manage events in our lives. None of us goes through life without encountering difficulty, heartache, loss and hurt along the way. I've noticed that the people who cope with obstacles best of all are those who realise one simple fact: that it's only life happening to them. When someone passes or you lose a friend, or a job, life is not being evil to you. It's just part of the journey.

## Take responsibility for your actions

If you can learn to see everything that happens – good or bad – as part of the same jigsaw, you will find it easier to cope with whatever life throws at you. While you cannot be rid of sadness or pain, you can control it by taking the right attitude. I have 'read' for people from all walks of life and I have come to the conclusion that the ones who look like they are 'cruising' through life do not necessarily have an easy time of it; they are just people who accept their circumstances and then actively deal with them. They don't sit around waiting for life to get 'good' again; they make an effort to turn things round. Even when things don't go their way, they don't blame outside forces, they just accept it. As a lovely old lady of my acquaintance used to say, 'It is what it is.' No more. No less.

One day I sat down with a lady called Linda to do a one-to-one reading. She had one of those delightful, bubbly personalities that immediately engages you but she seemed to be a little unsure. However, she was still very determined to go through with the reading.

Almost as soon as Linda sat down, I felt a male energy. It was very strong, almost overpowering. I knew this man had passed over in his forties, yet he seemed extremely young in a childish way.

'This man seems very close to you, Linda.'

'It's my brother. We used to love messing around like kids even when we got older.'

The message became clearer. I took a breath: it wasn't going to be an easy one for Linda.

'He knew that his time in this world was limited. He says it ended sooner than he thought.'

Linda had tears in her eyes. 'Yes,' she said softly.

'He enjoyed a drink in life, didn't he?'

I knew it was a question that didn't need to be asked: the answer was obvious. Linda became quite upset and was struggling to hold back her tears. At this point I felt for her but

I had to ignore my own emotions. I asked if she wanted me to continue.

She was struggling. 'Yes please, do go on.'

'I think he enjoyed rather a few too many.'

Now I was seeing rather a lot of bottles and I also felt the crunch of glass under my feet. I had a worry that these memories might contain violent episodes, but was quickly reassured that they didn't.

Linda's brother then said, 'I always loved Linda because she was the one who never judged me.'

'I would never ever do that,' she said. 'He's my brother.'

It was obvious how close these two had been.

The spirit started to show me an older figure, his father. I thought that maybe he too had passed over, but Linda explained that he was still alive. I concentrated harder – the man wanted me to pass on a special message to his father.

'It was my fault,' he said. 'Tell Dad it was my fault. Dad wanted to blame the world, but it really it was all my own fault.'

'I'll tell him,' said Linda, dabbing her eyes with a tissue.

My communicator continued with calm thoughts.

'He's telling me that he misses you but he's happier now. He's safe and the demons have gone. He no longer needs to hide from them.'

His final piece of evidence that his spirit had survived was to tell her that he approved of the picture of him she had placed above the fireplace: she had touched it up to hide the fact that he was going bald!

'Well I like to remember him that way.'

During my readings, I believe it's important to speak to the sitter – in this case Linda – as little as possible beforehand. During the reading all I really want them to say to me is 'yes' or 'no' so I know whether they understand what I am saying or not. However, after the reading I'm always curious to know exactly what the person is thinking and what they have taken away from the communication.

Linda was surprisingly relaxed as she explained to me that her brother had gone through a great deal of stress in his life. He had become an alcoholic at a relatively early age, eventually dying from alcohol-related disease. 'Dad still can't talk about it. He never understood alcohol addiction and kept looking for other reasons. He was always blaming other people.'

The truth was that his son had chosen his path in life and it was his own fault. Linda understood that what her father felt was usual. It is natural for a parent to want to overlook their child's faults. But here was Linda's brother saying not only was he OK; more importantly he was now accepting full responsibility for his actions and decisions when he was physically on this earth.

I'm pleased that Linda's brother was able to communicate how he now felt but it would have been even better for him and his family if he'd been able to take that responsibility early on.

We have no problem accepting responsibility on the most basic level: If you knock over a glass of wine then you are responsible for staining the tablecloth. We are able to accept the responsibility of paying a mortgage but without wanting to sound flippant, this is the small stuff. What we all need to think about is how many times we try to get out of being responsible for the events that happen in our lives. How often do we say, 'It was just *circumstance* or *bad luck* or *fate*'? In my experience the people who resort to this are also more likely to sit around and wait for something good to happen instead of actively seeking their happiness.

Please understand I'm not saying that in this big, complex world of ours we can control everything that happens to us. Of course there are events that happen in a person's life beyond their control such as bereavement, illness and emotional or physical abuse. The most important thing is how we move forward once the event has happened. Whether what has happened to us is fair or not is irrelevant. We are now responsible for dealing with that event and turning a negative experience into a positive, thus gaining strength through it. I'm not saying it's easy – of course it's not – but life is here to test us in all sorts of ways, good and bad. Once we accept – as Linda's brother finally did – that the buck stops with us and only us, then we are ready to move forward. The longer we rage against what has happened, the longer we will be stuck in the moment that has passed. That's more precious time we are taking off our life on this side.

It is so much easier to adopt a victim mentality and blame others for our problems. You don't have to look far to see we live in a society where being a victim is encouraged rather than discouraged. Look at how much space the media devote to stories of people who have been wrongly done by; tricked by their insurance company, ignored by their bank and swindled by their mechanic. Well, life isn't fair and things will go wrong – yes, even for me! However, I don't see myself as a victim when I choose a holiday that doesn't turn out to be ideal: I just think 'Oh, well that wasn't so good, I won't go there again.' The responsibility was mine because I chose. I was not a helpless victim forced to look at glossy holiday brochures! You are not a victim because as I said at the start of this chapter, you have the freedom to choose and that means you can choose how to react to events. Remember, this is all part of life. Life is not all about receiving good things; rather it's how you react to its problems and challenges that makes you who you are.

The wonderful thing about speaking with Linda after her reading was the realisation that she really did understand this. Her brother had died young from a disease that had destroyed his life and placed terrible burdens on their family. And her father was still unable to deal with what happened. Linda had not resorted to saying it was unfair. She had not sought to blame external circumstances such as her brother's schooling or social crowd. No matter how cruel it was to lose her brother at a relatively young age, she knew she had to tackle it head on and deal with it. The bad things that had happened within the family were not her 'doing', but how she dealt with the situation since, was. Linda was letting go of the past and doing her best to steer her life forwards. I knew that she would pass on the message from her brother to her father, and that it would help in his grieving process.

When I'm involved in giving psychic predictions I'm obviously picking up on important vibrations. However, the way in which you interpret those findings and what you choose to believe is entirely up to you. You get to choose how you will use those predictions to go forward.

## You have nothing to fear but fear itself

It is something I myself had to learn. In my early twenties I was managing a carpet store. It was a family-run business and I had worked there for several years. Meanwhile I knew that I had psychic ability. I'd been sitting in a basic development group for a few years, but as a practising medium I was doing very little. Many people have psychic tendencies, but do not always choose to develop them. Those that do decide, do so at different ages and stages in their lives. As it is not something that can be taught through conventional courses and study, development is done in a person's free time – which invariably needs to be financed by another job or profession. A person with psychic or mediumistic tendencies will join a development circle for several years before they would dare take money for their services, and there are not many who can then make a living from mediumship alone.

Back to the carpet store: one day an elderly couple came in to buy a carpet. The people who worked there were pretty rude about people who came into the shop to discuss having new carpets fitted but would never go through with it. They used to call them 'WOTS' – 'Waste of Timers'. I looked up from my paperwork to find that all of my employees had amazingly disappeared at the same time and I was left to deal with this elderly gentleman and his wife in a wheelchair. I spent a large part of the morning showing them every available sample shade of red in the warehouse but I confess that I didn't expect them to actually buy. So I was surprised when they asked me round the next day to measure their flat for the carpets.

The next day I arrived and put my briefcase down in their lounge and got my tape measure out. At that moment a voice came to me and said, 'Tell this man that you know that he uses this room for séances.' I tried to ignore it, but the voice just got louder.

So I turned to the old man and said, 'Look, you can tell me to leave and you will probably think I am quite mad, but you conduct séances in this room, don't you?'

'Yes.' He didn't look surprised but asked me how I knew.

I just came out with the truth. 'Well look, this voice has just told me.'

He grabbed me by the arm and rushed me into the kitchen

where his wife was sitting in her wheelchair and he said, 'Tell my wife what you just told me.' Before I could utter a word she looked me in the eye and said, 'Oh yes, we knew you were coming.'

I was a bit freaked out by this (most conversations with customers start with 'Do you take milk?' and 'How many sugars?') so I didn't take it seriously. 'Yes. Of course you knew I was coming, because you invited me to measure the flat.'

Ignoring me she continued, 'We've been running a medium-istic physical phenomena circle for the last twenty-five years with my husband's mum, but since her death have continued sitting once a month with another trance medium. He told us that a young man would come to us during the course of his work, he would identify himself as a medium and we were to take the responsibility of developing him. So, would you come and sit with us?' If you think that light came forth from the heavens and angels sang *hallelujah* then I'm afraid nothing could be further from the truth. My gut feeling was to run for my life, but as I went home that evening there was something bothering me. Why wasn't I pursuing my mediumship? Why wasn't I going for it and making it happen? Maybe if I went along and met a new set of people, people who were prepared to experiment with physical phenomena, I might find something new and exciting in my life.

Most of all I realised that perhaps the reason I was not developing into a professional full-time medium was fear – the fear of failure. It is only human nature to be afraid of failing at something, but it must not be allowed to stop you improving your life. As a young boy I can clearly remember listening to elderly friends of my parents or relatives talk about the things they wished they could have done. Like all young people I never really stopped to think about whether I would ever feel regret because I didn't take an opportunity. Now I'm older I too have to face the reality that I will regret what I haven't done rather than celebrating what I have done. You will never have a life free of regret but you can have a life where you have much to celebrate instead. The way to do that is to stop talking about what you should be doing and just do it! 'But,' I hear you say, 'there isn't a right time.' Absolute rubbish. There is never a right time. The right time is the time you decide to act. Gather your courage and go out there and do it!

## Buy your ticket to life now

There's an old joke about the guy who complains to God that he never wins the lottery, only to have God suggest to him that he should actually buy a ticket! We can only achieve what we want from life by acting on our desires, not by ignoring our issues or wishing things were different. This can mean confrontation. But if something is important to us we must tackle it. My good friend and fellow medium Tony Stockwell and I read for families who were parents of British soldiers (Military Police) who had been killed on duty in Iraq. Some of the families are currently challenging the Ministry of Defence over the 'official' version of events. Their chances of success in taking on the government are not high, but these families are determined in their struggle, for they know that they will only fail if they stop in the face of their difficulties. These people, rather than asking, 'How can we take on the government?' bravely say, 'How can we not?' It has become their duty and life's work to seek the truth. Now you and I both know they are up against it, but that doesn't stop them trying. And that's the attitude you should have. The people who say you can't change your career or sell up and go and live abroad are only people like you. Listen to yourself rather than to them. After all, the only person who understands your inner needs is you.

I've been talking as if we only have one life, but what if we are given the chance to have more than one life? People often ask me my thoughts on the subject of reincarnation. Despite experiencing and seeing many psychic phenomena over the years I am not 100 per cent convinced of the arguments for reincarnation. My personal opinion is that a spirit moves on. I believe in a creating force or God whose world is a constant source of new creation, not just reincarnation.

I am certainly not knocking anyone who believes in it and plenty of people do. There have been several tests carried out on both adults and children (often but not always under hypnosis), who have proved able to recall different lives in extreme detail. If one believes that people have led past lives then obviously one can believe in the potential to live additional ones.

Nevertheless, the fact that you believe in reincarnation does not absolve you from living your present life profitably on this side. You are still responsible for your own actions, whether you come back in another form or not. The pitfall for many people who believe in reincarnation is that they will be so convinced of the value of the life they are yet to have they will fail to make the most of this one. It is all too easy to say I was nobody last time and I'm sure I'll be a king or princess the next time round! The bottom line is that whatever you believe on this issue, you will only have one life as 'you'. By 'you' I mean the way you know and understand yourself today. If you believe in reincarnation you must assume that you will have no memory of the life you lead at the moment. Therefore you must deal with the world you live in and the life you lead today, not rely on further incarnations. Whatever your beliefs you must fully engage with the issues of your world, before you devote your life to engaging with the issues of others. Also remember that if you are reincarnated, whatever you become will still have your personality and characteristics, no matter what form it takes. You cannot shake off who you are.

## Lead a life: don't wait for one to happen to you

- Our lives are short and are ours to make the best of. We have to live them in the most productive way possible and not just wait for things to happen to us – because they won't.
- The buck stops with you. You are responsible for everything that happens in your life. Even if you have not directly caused or created it, you can choose how you progress.
- You are not a victim: you are a person who has choices in life just like any other person. Therefore if you become a victim it's because you have chosen to be one.
- Although you cannot determine everything in your life, you can decide how to deal with things that happen to you. You can choose your attitude.
- Enjoy each moment for what it is, no matter how small. Even if you believe in reincarnation, you have only this life as you. The present is a wonderful gift.
- Fear of failure is no excuse for not taking a step in life. It is a reason to find the courage within yourself.

# 2.

# Believing: the power of positive thinking

*'Most folks are about as happy as they make up their minds to be.'*

**ABRAHAM LINCOLN**

Not so long ago a friend of mine pointed out how curious it was that both psychics and chefs were enjoying a great deal of popularity on television. 'I've got a great idea,' she said, 'why not combine the two with a police series – a drama with a detective whose sidekick is a psychic chef! Then you'd have a real winner.'

'Perhaps the reason they're so popular is that they both encourage us to improve our well-being and therefore our happiness,' I suggested. She nodded absentmindedly – perhaps she was dreaming up plots for her new police series?

I see what I do as being of immense practical value to people. If I had to sum up the benefits of psychic mediums I would say that we try as far as possible to improve a person's state of mind. That doesn't mean we are telling them what they want to hear but instead directing them to perhaps think or act in a certain way. I truly believe we can change the way we think about things and in doing so add meaning and purpose to our lives. In other words it is not what life throws at us but our approach in dealing with it that can count for much more. The biggest difference between people is not the colour of their skin, the size of their bodies, or whether they are rich or poor; it is their attitude to life that separates each and every one of them. I believe that with the aid of positive thinking anyone can overcome all sorts of barriers in their lives. When I use the phrase 'positive thinking' I don't mean it in a 'think rich and you will grow rich' kind of way. Positive thinking can be a very deep and healing experience, as the following reading demonstrates.

A few years back at a private 'one-to-one' I remember suddenly being overcome with a great wave of sadness. I knew that I was about to receive a communication from a person who had died young and in tragic circumstances. The lady I was reading for was called Anilka and the information I received from the spirit world was detailed and remarkable.

I began to detect the presence of a very good-looking woman moving close to me. She gave me a warm grand-motherly feeling and seemed from a bygone age.

'She tells me that you are very accomplished in tradition-al cooking – that you still make things in the traditional way.'

I began to feel strongly that Anilka had taken on the role of being the matriarch responsible for gathering her family and providing for them. Then the spirit started to show me other details.

'I see soldiers in two different types of uniform. I don't know if this is symbolic or whether I'm being shown something actual,' I said. 'There is a brick wall and a soldier or soldiers in one uniform on one side, and as I go to the other side of this brick wall I see a soldier or soldiers in another uniform.'

I asked her if her family had been victims of a military conflict. She replied that this was correct and I suddenly felt a very sharp pain in my leg. 'Who was the man who was shot in the leg?' I knew that this man was spirit side, but had not died from his wound. 'This man your grandmother is referring to was shot in the leg because he was trying to protect the innocent.'

The spirit continued with her message. 'This woman is showing me the image of almost being on her knees, almost praying for peace. She is giving me this memory of sadness that she did not remain or survive life on this side long enough to see the family be reconnected again after they were separated.' I had to ask a question. 'Would you understand that she had to bury one of her own, herself?'

Anilka paused for some time. 'Yes,' she eventually replied. 'And I actually mean dig the grave, put the body in and fill it with earth, and she had to do it herself. This grave has never been properly marked and that's why the memory has to be kept alive.'

The lady had one final message and this was two-fold. Firstly that there was a young boy with stunning eyes in the family who must be taught in his native language and secondly that Anilka had to write the family story down for the benefit of the children so that it would never be forgotten. After the reading, amid much emotion and many tears, the complete story came out. The message was from Anilka's grandmother. Anilka told me, 'They shot my grandfather in the leg and the bullet stayed there until he died when I was eleven.'

The war in question took place between Armenia and Turkey at the beginning of the last century and resulted in the genocide of a significant part of the Armenian population. Many family members had eventually managed to flee from the Turkish troops and the subsequent genocide, but they were scattered across many countries in the Middle East.

Anilka continued, and told me one of the saddest things I have ever heard in my life.

'When my grandparents fled from Turkey towards Iraq, they saw that all young women and children were being systematically raped and then buried alive by the Turkish soldiers. So they took the decision to kill their own young daughter rather than let her suffer this fate. Her grandmother buried the girl with her own hands, and to this day the family never knew the name of the girl or where she was buried. Although her current experiences in the present day United Kingdom are light years away from this history, Anilka has never forgotten it. Yet what struck me about her was not her bitterness, sadness or anger but how she was trying to move on with her life.

'I do my best to speak in the Armenian language at every available opportunity to my nephew – he is the boy with beautiful eyes.'

I had to ask how the family had coped following such trauma, and she said, 'They did not all manage to cope. Some were able to rebuild their lives, others did not. Some chose to forget but I think they are just holding on to the past.'

It seemed that the ones who had rebuilt their shattered lives with the most success were those who had tried to salvage some sort of meaning – something positive – from the whole tragedy. Anilka's personal reaction to the reading was the realisation that she had to write this story down for the sake of her children and grandchildren. History was beyond her control, but her reaction to that history was not. What this story confirmed to me was that it is possible to give meaning and purpose to your life by changing the way you think about things. And most important-ly, it is possible to go on living.

## You are what you think

The majority of our problems will most certainly not be on a par with those of the people affected by the events in the previous story. However, that story does provide a reminder that even if history conspires against us, we are not doomed. Communications from the spirit world are valuable reminders that we have a responsibility to survive and to use the sadness and tragedy in our lives as reasons to find something positive. Just because negative things happen in our lives, that does not mean we should take a negative position.

The reason I sound so passionate about all this is because there was one event in my early professional life that almost ended my career as a medium and shattered my faith in my own development. The only reason that I am still a practising medium today is due to the healing power of positive thinking. Remember in the first chapter I told you about the elderly couple that had come into the carpet shop. I was invited to join their development circle and eventually accepted. A development group is the first port of call for anyone who thinks that they might possess a paranormal power or experience supernatural phenomena. The best way to find information about joining one is to make contact with a local spiritualist church or small psychic development group who will direct you appropriately. The development circle itself is a small group of people who meet to evaluate and ultimately to develop a person's psychic ability. Although I always knew I was 'different' when growing up, it wasn't until the late 1980s when I was in my mid twenties that I started to take this ability more seriously.

I need to explain one other point here. Mediumship can be divided up into what is called physical mediumship and spiritual mediumship. Spiritual mediumship is what most people reading this book know of today due to its exposure and popularity on television. A medium communicates with his senses with the spirit world and passes on messages for loved ones still living. Physical mediumship is when the medium tries to manifest spirits from the spirit world using physical phenomena such as inviting the spirit to move objects (such as a table) or inviting the spirit to communicate by using a cone-shaped instrument illuminated at the top and bottom often called a 'trumpet' or causing an *etherealisation* – whereby the spirit appears in a tangible but not physical sense. This might all sound weird and wonderful for those not acquainted with psychic phenomena, so as always feel free to check it out from other sources, attend a demonstration if you can and then make your mind up.

The actual process is simple. The physical medium is secured to a chair. The observers form a circle. Various objects such as a child's soft toy, a small musical instrument, some crystals or minerals are left in front of the medium. The lights are turned off and songs or prayers are recited to enhance the ambient vibrations. If all goes well, the medium goes into a trance and allows spirits to cross over and manipulate the objects. When the demonstration is over the medium comes out of their trance and the ties that bind them should be untouched. These forms of physical mediumship have historically proved to be controversial. To avoid dealing with such difficulties, the Spiritualist movement largely divorced itself from such mediumship fifty years ago.

As a young medium I began to explore physical mediumship. For one so young and new to it, I achieved some spectacular results and manifestations. The trouble was I began to believe my own press and publicity. I actually began to think that I was in charge of controlling these physical manifestations from the spirit world, rather than considering that sometimes it might actually be the other way round. Over the course of about two years I demonstrated for a closed circle group called the Noah's Ark Society (NAS), and was persuaded to give occasional public demonstrations. In order to protect my personal life I was given the name of 'Lincoln'. NAS differed slightly from the accepted view of the Spiritualist movement: it felt that one of its missions was to try and see this highly evidential and precious form of mediumship emerge once again and become available to all people.

So in November 1992, I was talked into giving a more public demonstration of my physical mediumship. There were many at that time including myself who felt that it was really too early in my development of this form of mediumship to be allowing so many outside sitters to attend. There was quite a lot of pressure placed upon me based upon my past results and to be honest I did feel quite stressed about it all. The truth was that I had a feeling things were going to go wrong that day. However, I didn't want to let people down, and if I'm honest, my ego was getting the better of me! After being secured to a Windsor style chair using 300 lb breaking strain cable ties, the light switches were turned off, boxed over and secured with duct tape. From the beginning the sounds and manifestations from the other side that evening were unsophisticated and unrefined. Approximately twenty minutes into the proceedings the main light came on for about five seconds. Those attending claimed I was standing in a trance-like state holding a trumpet in the middle of the room. I fell to the floor in a state of confusion and shock and was escorted out.

I remember very little of these proceedings, but witnesses said that at the time I was in great distress and in considerable pain with bruising and burn marks to my stomach. Unfortunately this was nothing compared to the furore that was caused in psychic circles. By not controlling the spirit phenomena I had let many people down, most of all those who had helped me develop. Although the broken cable ties (which cannot be undone by pulling once tightened) were tested by a polymer expert in the materials department of Newcastle University showing that I could not have cut them on my own without cutting my hands and feet, I was distressed by the bad publicity generated and the fact that I had provided many sceptics with the ammunition they needed to attack what I loved most.

It was obvious that I was not as good a medium as I'd thought and I needed to go away and strengthen my mediumship. Together with the NAS I decided that I would no longer demonstrate publicly until my spirit guides gave explicit instructions to resume. In psychic circles this of course became a big story. *Psychic News* reported extensively on the event and I felt hurt hounded and confused. The question was, how should I react to all this? I won't pretend that I wasn't worried. Maybe I was not meant to be a medium? Maybe I had squandered the gift I had been blessed with? If I was destined to be a medium then perhaps I had thrown it all away by allowing my integrity to be questioned? After several months of searching and despite the support of the NAS I had to confront the fact that I was becoming what I thought – 'a failure'. With my future in the balance I realised that I had to make a choice. Either I believed in what I did or I didn't. I had to make this experience into a positive one. I had to use this experience to grow and give me new purpose.

Replacing the negative thoughts and experiences connected to a bad episode with positive ones does not mean pretending that the negative doesn't exist, but it does mean changing your attitude and viewing your life path in a different way. As a result I have never avoided talking about this subject and have done so publicly on many occasions. I now employ it during lectures as a warning to students not to push the development of their mediumship too fast. I have treated it as an experience that has helped me improve rather than let it ruin me. I used it to re-evaluate myself and to work harder. As a result I am a better and more sensitive medium for having undergone this experience. To connect back to what was said at the beginning of the chapter, this event and its initial aftermath was something I could not control, but I had to learn to control my reaction to it. A failure was turned into a positive learning experience that enabled me to grow both personally and professionally.

## Project positivity and your life will improve

The people who cope best with life's lows and the negative feelings that result from them accept that these are all just part of life. They don't push them away but accept that this has been dealt to them and they will get over it and move on. Almost certainly by taking this attitude, they will be stronger and better for it when they do. One way of doing this is to ask yourself how much something will matter in the future. You may be heart-broken about a love affair that has gone wrong now but ask yourself how you will feel in a year. We have a wonderful ability to heal and chances are you will be feeling a million times better – if you make the effort. Remember what I said in chapter 1 about choosing your life.

We choose whether our reactions to an event are positive or negative, enthusiastic or dull, active or passive. Positive think-ing means welcoming into our mind thoughts, words and images that are helpful to growth, success and accomplish-ment. It means changing our expectations to those of positive and encouraging results. An optimistic mind anticipates joy, contentment, health and a successful outcome to every avail-able situation and action. Whatever the mind expects, it will find. The truth is that positive and negative thinking are both contagious. All of us affect, in one way or another, the world we interact in. This happens instinctively through our body lan-guage, which communicates these internal feelings. You do not have to be a psychic sensitive to pick up on these signals. I find these rules work for me when communicating with those on both sides of life, and I continually try to focus on positive thoughts when reading for people. Sometimes it can be diffi-cult to understand the messages coming through to me, for like any person I can only interpret what is being said to me in the light of what I know, and have experienced and understood in my life.

Sometimes I can have a spirit connect to me and there is a signal or piece of information that I have never experienced. It becomes very hard to recognise what the message is about, or what the feelings and the imagery mean. In such cases where it might take me more time and effort to adjust to what is being communicated, I try to focus on thoughts of encouragement and accomplishment. Spirits definitely seem more willing and able to help me if I am radiating positive energy.

### Exercise:
## Changing your attitude

No matter what your circumstances are at the present moment, try these exercises in helping you to think in a more positive manner. Expect only favourable results and circumstances will change accordingly. It may take some time for the changes to take place, but eventually they will.

- First of all place two pictures in front of you. Try to concentrate on only one of them. Block out the other picture even though it is staring you in the face.
- Once you have mastered this, try the same exercise in your imagination. The idea here is to train your brain to concentrate only on one thing. If the image of the picture you are not trying to think about pops up then replace it with the image of the other picture.
- The final stage is to replace the images with thoughts. Every time a negative thought or outlook pops up in your head you must learn to replace it with a positive

one. Perseverance and practice will eventually teach your mind to think positively and ignore negative thoughts.

## So now ...

- Look in the mirror and define your current short- and long-term goals. Think about what opportunities exist for improving your life by achieving these goals.
- Think about what might motivate you to achieve these goals. Try to find inspiration and think creatively about the issues that are important to you.
- Negative thoughts, words and attitudes you might have about reaching these goals will lead to negative and unhappy moods and actions which are not conducive to success. Replace any negative thoughts with positive ones based on your creative motivations and expected rewards from achieving your goals.
- If you find yourself struggling to replace your negative thoughts with positive ones, do not give up, but remember your two pictures. If you can replace one image in your mind with another, then you can also eventually replace negativity and pessimism with the beneficial, good and happy thoughts that also exist in your mind.

## And remember ...

- You must always believe in yourself and your abilities. If you do not believe in yourself you cannot expect anyone else to. Always try to exhibit self-esteem and radiate confidence.
- Develop a strategy for dealing with problems. No-one's

life runs entirely smoothly, so look for solutions. Try to look at failure and problems as blessings in disguise or platforms to learn and grow from.

• Never give up. Always expect success. If success does not come initially, then try again. You must ignore any feelings of laziness or a desire to quit. If you persevere, not only will you achieve your goal but you will also transform the way your mind thinks and find it easier to succeed in achieving future goals.

When I said that I believe 'you are what you think', I didn't just mean on a psychological level, I believe it can also affect the way your body performs as well. Imagine it is a boiling hot day and you have been on the train with no air conditioning. There are no seats available and you do not even have room to read a newspaper. Sweat is beginning to run down your neck and you feel more than hot and bothered. Now imagine the cold drink that awaits you at the end of the journey (I'll leave your actual dream drink for the imagination!). I suspect that like most people your reaction to this scenario is to salivate at the prospect of enjoying the liquid refreshment. The things you think can actually affect the way your body reacts. Normally a person would only salivate if they smelled a delicious food or saw something they really wanted to taste, but here a simple thought has prompted the same powerful reaction.

Here's another example, which actually happened to me when I went away for a few days to concentrate on writing this book. Imagine you are alone in a room, it is night time and you hear a faint creak coming from a floorboard in another room. You are pretty sure it cannot be an intruder but I'll bet all sorts of scenarios rush through your head and the chances are that you will experience what thriller writers describe as the hairs rising on the back of your neck! Once again it is the thoughts generated by your imagination that are affecting your body and its physical reactions. In this case strong thoughts about danger and what steps you will take to protect yourself and the house will cause adrenalin to pump through your body thus raising your energy level.

## Dealing with negative people

Well it's all well and good if all we have to worry about is our own attitudes, but what about all the negative people who invade our lives and make us feel bad? How can we deal with them? Let me tell you about Elaine, who had spent over twenty years looking after her mother Joyce.

We were having a private sitting and when Joyce came through it was clear that she did not see her final years on the earth as pleasant ones. She was one of these people – and there are many of them – who could not accept her old age and the passing of her youth and vitality. So what had she done? She had decided to take out her insecurities and regrets by being cruel to her well-meaning daughter, Elaine.

When Elaine arrived at my house in the spring of 1991 she would have been in her late forties. She was tidy in appearance and I was struck by a lady who had all the potential to be glamorous but in her ill-fitting raincoat and tied-back hair she did not do herself justice. I had the sense that this lady had been through something that had affected her self-esteem.

'Hello,' she said as she shyly looked down at the floor.

'Please, sit down, Elaine, and we'll begin if you're ready.'

She smiled nervously. 'Thank you.'

We sat down and very quickly I became aware of the spirit presence of her mother Joyce. The story began to unfold rather like a film playing in my head: it was a tale of Elaine looking after her mother. This was not going to be one of my easier communications. Already I knew it would be a communication of regrets, sadness and ultimately reconciliation and release.

'There is music and I see dancing. Who is dancing, Elaine?'

Still not looking up, she replied, 'That's my mother. Dad was a session musician and Mum was a successful dancer when she was younger.'

It seemed that Joyce combined her work with the dance troupe with raising Elaine, her only daughter. Her life was pretty near perfect.

'Your parents were very creative and successful, Elaine.'

'They were, but I wasn't,' she said softly. 'I think they were disappointed in me because I couldn't play music or dance.'

I sensed that here was a lady who had not had much encouragement from her parents, suffering as a result, and I said as much.

'Well, not exactly, but when I did well at school and then did well in my nursing studies, they were not really interested.'

I really felt for her. The one thing every child needs is encouragement and praise. Poor Elaine had virtually been ignored because her parents could not see what she was good at. Sadly Ted, Joyce's husband, passed away just shortly before he was due to retire  and  within the next few years  Joyce fell victim to crippling arthritis.

'That must've been tough on her, having been a dancer.'

'It was tough on me,' said Elaine, almost whispering.

Being a dutiful daughter Elaine began to call in frequently on the way home from work  to check that her mother was OK.

At this point she had been established for several years as a staff nurse at the local hospital and felt she was the best person to attend to her mum's needs.

Over the course of the following eighteen months, Joyce became less and less able and was obviously in a great deal of pain with her arthritis. As people often are when they're suffering she was not in a good mood; however, this went further.

'I sense she was very uncompromising towards you.'

'Umm yes ... actually she was a bit nasty at times but I'm sure she didn't mean it. She was in so much pain.'

'I know she upset you, Elaine.'

Elaine was trying not to show her pain. She had tears in her eyes as she explained that her mother became quite bitter and used to pick on her about her appearance, constantly telling her that 'no man would ever want to marry such a sad looking creature.' The fact that her daughter was exhausted didn't seem to enter her head. She just continued to abuse her. Poor Elaine was indeed exhausted and had just enough energy to go home to her little flat, feed her cat and collapse into bed, always fearing that the phone would ring with news that something had happened to her mother. Apparently the insults from her mother lasted right up until Joyce's death. Even though Elaine loved her mother, it had all been too much and now, amongst other things, she had a very low opinion of herself.

Here we were three years on and as Elaine sat with me, I passed on the message of regret and apology from her mother.

'She says she's sorry for being so ungrateful for all the love and support but also for making you feel so bad about yourself.'

Elaine said nothing. She just nodded in her sweet, shy way.

'She wants you to know that despite all the terrible things

she said to you, that she never meant it. She was proud of your achievements; she just could not see beyond her own fear and regret of getting old.'

Elaine responded, 'I know that. I used to keep telling myself that she was struggling with getting older.'

'She wants you to accept her love and her apology and to be proud of yourself.'

Elaine burst into tears, yet as I watched her I realised that this sitting, although painful, would produce a positive outcome. So often in life we can become victims of another person's dissatisfaction with themselves. We absorb all their negativity for them until we actually believe we are unworthy. Somehow we need to rise above it. That may mean, in some situations, cutting yourself off from negative people. For example you may have a friend who takes it upon herself to spend much of her time criticising everyone except herself. We all know people like that. As well as making people around them feel unworthy, they can also pass on their negative attitude so that without realising it, you become one of those critical people. In my view you don't want to spend too much time with someone like that. Life is far too short. If you find yourself around people who make you feel bad about yourself, you need to tell them that this is happening. Explain that you want to feel good and they are not helping you. Whether it's a work environment or relationship, if it can't or won't change, then I would advise you to leave it behind.

I met Elaine once more a few years later. It was in the spring of 1998. A very attractive woman with beautifully styled clothes and hair tapped me on the shoulder while I was in Brighton shopping. 'Thank you for the sitting. It really helped me.' I told her it was my pleasure and I was glad to see how radiant she looked. Incidentally she was with a very handsome middle-aged gentleman who she informed me was her new husband.

## Be positive towards others

One way of feeling good towards ourselves – and doing our bit to create a better world – is to shift our sights to other people. You might be feeling rubbish but ask the checkout girl in the supermarket, whose job is fairly mindless, how she's feeling and you might be able to spread a little positivity. Her reaction is likely to make you feel better and in this way you can spread a bit more light in the world. Caring for others is also a way of conquering our own fears. If for example you are with children, then it is easier to forget you are afraid of the dark or heights or hate the rain etc. when you are making sure that everyone is present and correct and not feeling down or frightened. By helping others and sensing their appreciation, our confidence is increased and our fear subsides.

As participants in my demonstrations will know, I start every sitting I ever do, whether for two people or two thousand, with the same ritual. I always ask my listeners to uncross their arms, to open their minds and to think positively. Spirits, in my experience, come through on a vibration of happiness and love, not misery and negativity. I always ask people to uncross their arms so that they are sitting in an 'open' fashion and not defensively – allowing the positive energies to emanate from their solar plexus. But most importantly I always ask people to pray that the person next to them gets a message, and in that way, with everybody praying for the success of the strangers around them, an incredible energy and atmosphere is created.

There is an old proverb that states, 'He who is rich is he who is happy with what he owns.' How true this is. Inner happiness is not determined by material circumstances or sensual gratification. It depends on our state of mind. We must be positive and happy with what we have. A lack of something we desire is no barrier to the possession of noble thoughts and as long as we are striving for these our lives will have more meaning.

A positive attitude will help you to cope more easily with the ups and downs of life. As a way of life, it will help generate constructive changes for making your life happier, brighter and more successful. It will help you to be optimistic and expect the best to happen. It will not only affect you and the way you look at the world, but also your personal environment and the people around you.

## Develop a more positive attitude

- Remember you are what you think. Choose to be happy. You cannot choose what happens to you but you can choose how to react to it. Try to look on the bright side of life and find reasons to smile and laugh more often.

- By projecting positivity you will encourage it to come to you. People will sense that you are worth being around and you will attract good things.

- Don't think of negative occurrences as something abnormal. Treat them as a normal part of life and then they will be manageable.

- Associate yourself with happy, positive people. The truth is that you are affected by your surroundings and this includes the people that you mix with. Whether at work or in your social life, look for positive people to associate with. That might mean getting rid of negative people in your life.

- Think about what you can do to make others feel positive. You will be enthused and look at life differently when you realise that you can inspire and motivate other people.

# 3.

# Understanding: your family is not you

*'In each family a story is playing itself out, and each family's story embodies its hope and despair.'*

**AUGUSTE NAPIER**

'*We can choose our friends, but we can't choose our family.*' It kind of begs the question, 'Well, am I stuck with them no matter what?' You are stuck with them in the sense that you are related; however, that doesn't mean that your future is determined by what happens in your family. While some people are fortunate to grow up in a loving, harmonious family, others will struggle with the inevitable complex nature of family relationships and may want or need to get away. Families are as much a source of comfort as they are of tension. I know this because family issues form a large part of my work: of the messages I receive for people night after night easily 95 per cent of them are from a close family member and many of them refer to unfinished family business.

Whether it is approval for someone's choice of marriage partner, a particular child with behavioural issues or a financial matter left disputed, my life as a medium has shown me that there is 'nought as strange as family' and yet at the same time no matter how bad a relationship was between relatives, the one thing people want most out of a reading is for an unresolved family affair to be patched up. Unfortunately it is not always so simple. However, even if things do not work out, I don't believe that is an excuse for ruining the rest of your life with your family issues. You can choose to create your own 'family', something that has become a necessity in many people's lives as they live away from their biological families. This has meant developing a group of friends who function as a family by providing support and care for each other. Because they do it out of a desire to be together and not out of any biological obligation, there can often be a lot more give and take.

In any case you are not restricted by your upbringing. You may have to struggle to leave it behind but, as many famous and successful people have shown, your biology is not your destiny.

## A family is made up of individuals

I have seen much hurt and recrimination in families when someone has passed on and there has been no prior resolution of issues. One of the discussions I had with my editor was that although I have absolutely no desire to meddle in people's lives and tell parents how to bring up their children or children how to look after their parents, I do feel that years of experience in my profession have shown me that those who manage their family relationships successfully are far more mentally and emotionally prepared to cope after a loved one passes away.

Quite often it's the tensions between parents and children that create problems. When you become a parent you are not given an instruction book. Nobody tells you how to do it; you just have to work it out for yourself and make your mistakes along the way. Over the years I have learned that one of the hardest things for parents to do is understand that they do not own their children. I really believe this to be true. Children are a gift; they are in your care until they are able to care for themselves and then you must set them free. They should be loved for whatever they are and whatever they become, for it is that which will give them the foundations on which to build. Being loved and valued for our individuality is essential to our self-esteem and confidence. A child that feels it has its parents' blessing to follow a chosen path will be happier and better adjusted than one who is steered into a direction of the parents' choosing. This is often a hard pill to swallow for many parents. The following encounter is just one of many I've had on this subject.

The studio lights are hot and I am beginning to get tired and irritated. It's been a long day and I have one more episode of my television series, *6ixth Sense*, to film and we are running late. I look out into the studio audience and attempt to open my mind so I can be receptive to spirit communication. Soon my mind becomes aware of a spirit, a gentleman who wants to communicate with his son. I see boxing paraphernalia and I am guided towards a rather strong-looking, powerfully built man in the audience.

'Your father tells me you have a connection to boxing,' I say in a way that is tentative by my standards. Actually, going by the appearance of the guy, even I had to admit it was stating the bloody obvious!

'Yes,' he said, unsmiling. Hmm, was this going to be one of those dialogues where I only get one-syllable answers? I reminded myself not to judge my audience member unfairly.

During the next fifteen minutes a message unfolded that to this day highlights the importance of expressing love within a family, or any close-knit group for that matter. My communicator painted me a picture of having been a tough man in life. He was ex-military and one of those old school types who believe that children need to be disciplined. Boys in particular, he said, should be raised to stand up for themselves and be real men. Well, that was pretty clear then.

The man in the audience confirmed that it was indeed his father and explained the significance of the boxing.

'When I was younger I showed promise at boxing. I used to train quite hard and became quite good at it. Dad never approved.'

'Was it you or the boxing that he didn't approve of?'

'Mostly me. He always told me I just wasn't good enough to be a pro boxer. He kept telling me that.'

'That was obviously hard for you.'

'It just didn't make any sense to me,' he said. 'One minute he's saying you have to grow up and be a real man, and the next minute I'm being the tough man he wants but he doesn't like it.'

It certainly seemed the father had sent out mixed signals. Apparently he had also thought outward signs of love and affection to be a weakness and, frankly, rather girlie.

As the years went on the inability of the father to show love and affection to the son meant that the son's lack of love made him exactly the same. So a wall formed between them to the point where every meeting turned into an argument, especially after the son had his own family.

'My father used to tell me how to raise my own children, which pushed us further apart. I didn't feel that was OK, especially after the way he'd raised me,' he told me later.

As his father began to slip out of this life, the son tried to show compassion to his old dad but found it difficult. Every time he tried all he could hear in his mind were the words: 'Son, you are never gonna make it. Just give up.'

It was very gratifying for me to be able to pass on the message from the father that he knew his son had become a belted championship boxer and that he was an excellent father, both of which made him very proud indeed.

'It's a bit late,' said the son.

'But it's never too late,' I replied. The son nodded and I could see he was trying to take the message in the conciliatory way it was intended but it was very hard for him.

As a medium, I am always happy to pass on messages that are potentially the start of a healing process, but I do so wish that families would do it before someone passes to the other side. The need for parents and children to find favour, love and acceptance in each other's eyes is a powerful desire that accompanies us throughout our lives. It is not something we should be slaves to; adults should not live vicariously through their children and children are not beholden to follow their parents' ideology or lifestyle choice, but when it works and individuals can appreciate each other's differences, it's a wonderful thing. In particular I think about my own father's attitude to what I do. It has long been one of 'I don't really understand what you do, son, and I'm not sure I want to'. Yet one of the proudest moments in my life was when he came to see *The Three Mediums* (Derek Acorah, Tony Stockwell and myself) demonstrate together at the Hammersmith Apollo. The show was packed out with about three thousand people, and was being recorded for television. The mediumship was very good, if I say so myself, in no small part because of the incredible buzz created by such a large audience and the fact that the chemistry generated by the three mediums was so special. After the demonstration had finished, my father bowled up to Derek, Tony and myself and said, 'Brilliant show! You guys were fantastic, I don't believe a word of it, but it was incredible!'

It was one of the proudest moments of my life so far.

## Be open to change

I talked earlier about parents not owning their children. I believe the same philosophy applies to all of us. If we truly love the people in our lives, we will accept we cannot bind them to promises. Instead we all need to be open to growth and change according to circumstance.

In 2004 Bill and his wife Maureen came to see me for a private sitting at my home in Sussex. Around that time I had deliberately cut back on private sittings due to my other commitments in television as well as my tours and teaching engagements at my college in Sweden. However, there was something about the gentle, kind and polite tone of Bill's voice that made me feel that despite my schedule, I should see him and his wife for a sitting. It turned out to be one of those occasions when I am truly glad I followed my instinct.

You did not need to be psychic to be able to see that this charming, elderly couple sitting before me were very much in love. In this cynical age of ours I find it very endearing to see older couples holding hands, although I sensed they were doing it for support as well. I began to sense the spirit world connecting for them around me.

'I have a lady with me who is showing me her name is Beth.'

Almost instantly a tear came to Bill's eye. Maureen squeezed his hand.

'Be brave, love; it's what we came for,' she said to him.

'Beth is giving me a strong feeling of being connected to both of you but mostly you, Bill.'

'Yes, I understand.'

'She wants you to know she is very happy for you and also that she has no wish to hold you to a promise that neither of you should have made to one another.

'Beth is also telling me that this in no way demeans the love you and she had for each other.'

At this point, both Bill and Maureen began to weep and clutch each other even more tightly.

As is usual with a sitting at this point, I had little idea of the importance of these words to Bill and Maureen. As the sitting continued to unfold, it became apparent that Beth had been Bill's first wife, with whom he had enjoyed a long and happy marriage. Sadly they had not been able to have children and so they had focused a lot of their attention on one another. They were rarely separated and had run a small village post office and general store together. As they approached middle age they had promised one another several times that neither of them would ever marry again should anything happen to the other one. The result was that Bill had been left with the lasting impression that

Beth had very strong feelings that to marry was not just for life on this side but for eternity.

Sadly Beth started to become ill in her early sixties. Initially this manifested itself as headaches and tiredness. Like a lot of people she shunned suggestions she should go to the doctor's. Bill had tried to get her to her local GP but he couldn't. One day Bill returned home to find Beth unconscious on the kitchen floor. She was rushed to hospital and they found out that she had a brain tumour which was advanced and inoperable.

It turned out that Maureen had been her best friend since childhood.

'Bill needed help caring for her – he still had to keep working – so I was happy to do it since she was my friend.'

'She was not around long after the diagnosis,' said Bill. 'We only had six months.' Both Bill and Maureen were at her bedside in her final moments.

Bill and Maureen proved to be a great comfort to one another, each having lost such an important person in their life, but gradually as the pain of their grief subsided they realised that a warmth and love was developing between them. Three years after Beth's passing they were married.

Even though they had found love again with each other, both suffered terrible guilt that they had betrayed the memory of Beth by marrying.

'Our families and friends told us that Beth would be happy,' said Maureen, 'but I couldn't feel completely happy knowing Bill had promised her he would never marry again. I felt we were doing something wrong.'

'I've been having nightmares about it,' Bill confided.

It was a joyful experience for me to be able to convey the message that, from the perspective of her spirit existence, Beth was able to express her love for Bill and Maureen by showing that absolute and binding promises made in life were unimportant now she felt part of the bigger picture of greater existence.

In an ideal world we would all hope and pray we could keep such commitments made out of love, but we have to be honest enough and realistic enough to be open about how we honour our commitments to our loved ones.

## The way you behave influences others

This is quite a hard concept to get to grips with because it places the responsibility of the relationship on you rather than placing the blame on the other person. It is not your fault how someone has behaved towards you, but from now on, how you react to that behaviour is.

Everybody goes through life moderating their behaviour based on results. They do what works for them in helping them achieve their desired aims. If a child is given chocolate every time he cries, he will purposely cry because he knows he's going to get a sweetie every time he does it. Ditto every time a child gets chocolate for behaving well. These patterns carry on into our adult lives. If a company offers job promotion and bonuses in exchange for successful results at work, most people will be inspired to work harder. If the company ignores you even though you have performed well you will slack off because your behaviour is not being rewarded.

In exactly the same way, the people you are close to in your life have learned and understood your response patterns to their behaviour and will act accordingly. It's like when you shop in the same store all the time; the cashier will often let you know in advance if what you are looking for is in stock. Meanwhile you might know from previous responses that you should not ask about the health of the cashier's mother if you do not want to hear about her varicose veins in great detail! So, if there is an aspect of a relationship you feel needs changing then the first port of call is to change your response patterns. You have to re-invent the way other people react to you and treat you.

Almost all rifts in a family relationship follow the same basic pattern.

- First of all, there is a lack of communication between the two parties.
- This is followed by periods of accumulated anger. Each party reinforces their belief in their own side of the argument.
- Frustration sets in as one or both parties refuses to compromise.
- And finally indifference sets in as both parties learn to adjust to the new reality of the broken relationship. This indifference might continue indefinitely if neither party tries to or is prepared to mend the relationship.

If you have a family relationship in which you feel you are not being treated correctly, you must ask yourself what you are doing to reinforce that behaviour. Ask yourself, in what way can you modify your response to that behaviour that shows it will no longer be acceptable to you? (In the extreme and unpleasant case where someone is verbally or physically violent, it is definitely not the fault of the abused that this is happening, but it is the abused who must take the responsibility of getting out of such a relationship. By not leaving or refusing to ask for help from the authorities s/he is reinforcing the other person's behaviour and saying that it will continue to be put up with.

Remember that it doesn't matter what you threaten to do;

only what you actually do. If you threaten a wayward teen with a punishment and never deliver you are just reinforcing their existing behaviour. If you carry it through, then the other person learns that they will not get what they want by the first way, and they will be forced to change their behaviour to another. The hardest part is often exchanging the safety of being a victim (i.e. telling everybody how awful the other person is) with the risky strategy of re-negotiating the relationship and provoking a life change. Once again it all boils down to how much you care. If you don't then it is unfair to expect others to.

Luckily in all but the most tragic and extreme cases the parties themselves can solve the problem by agreeing to reassess their relationship and by asking themselves what they wish the new relationship to be like. As we said before, true connections are based on give and take and compromise – with both parties compromising for the greater good of the relationship. So it is worthwhile for the two sides to ask each other the following points.

1) Make sure you both agree on what the common good in the relationship is. (E.g. maybe you both agree that you hate shouting at each other or you both agree that you will do anything to safeguard the health of a particular family member.)

2) Agree and accept the fact that compromises must be made on both sides. Make sure everybody knows what these are.

3) If it doesn't work then renegotiate the terms of your relationship again.

## How well do you really know your family?

Sometimes, no matter what, we can never know someone in our family that well, as the following story explains.

'Who went to see the monkeys?'

Well no-one can say that being a psychic medium is not without its surreal moments! There is nothing like appearing on national television and asking an audience if anyone has a poignant history with some apes! What had started as a regular demonstration suddenly took an interesting turn when my spirit communicator told me that they were looking for someone who had been promised a trip to see the monkeys.

I heard giggles from the audience.

'I don't mean the pop group,' I said. 'I mean real monkeys!'

All very amusing, but I realised I'd have to concentrate a little harder if this reading was going to contain real emotional substance. I started to sense the name Adrienne in my head and I asked for confirmation.

'Who is Adrienne? Who is looking for Adrienne?'

I began to see the situation more clearly. I needed to find someone in my audience who was looking not for Adrienne but for a man called Adrian. In fact I needed two people. Sometimes these things are not straightforward.

A lady in one of the back rows put up her hand.

'My grandfather was called Adrian and he came from France. Does that help?'

I knew that this message could only be for her if she could relate to the fact that there had been some recent talk about looking into that side of the family. She told me that there were two people interested in undertaking the research and I knew I was on the right track.

'Your grandfather promised you he'd take you to see some

monkeys,' I said. There were more giggles from the audience, who were possibly wondering where this was going.

'No,' she replied, 'that was Adrian's son – my father.'

Now that I knew I was meant to be with this lady, the thoughts and images flowed quickly through my head.

'There was someone involved in the clothing industry. In particular, someone who was very connected with young ladies' fashion.' I paused for a few seconds, unsure as to how to describe the next image that had appeared in my mind. 'In fact I can see rows and rows of low-cut sequinned dresses.'

The lady went bright red and giggled. I asked her if she wanted me to continue and she laughed and said out loud what I was thinking.

'It's OK,' she said. 'I'd rather I said it! Apparently my father owned a strip club in London!'

'I'm also being told I've got a lady here called Vicky.'

'Yes,' she said, 'Vicky was my dad's first wife.'

Good! I knew now that my message was going to be relevant and important. 'Vicky would like to send her regards. She also says that your father was a very mysterious man. One never really knew what he was up to.'

While all this was going on I sensed another spirit, this time male, who was hovering in the background, not so much unable, but perhaps unwilling to come through and speak for himself. I realised that the entire preamble was to bring this new spirit forward in order to pass something on. I want to digress at this point and tell you what in my opinion truly separates a good medium from an average one. I'm not talking here about levels of accuracy; I'm talking about psychological understanding of human nature.

When a person passes over into the spirit world they essentially retain the same characteristics as they possessed in their earthly life. Some communicators for example are shy, while others are rude. Some speak sparely and to the point, others do not let a medium get a word in edgeways. But in addition to their speech patterns they also come through with their own character traits and personalities.

Some messages are very straightforward. A spirit comes through and explains clearly who they want to speak to and what they want to pass on. But most messages are like the everyday communications we share with the people who surround us. Beyond the words themselves one also has to understand the nuance and subtleties of the complete meaning.

A good medium is one who can understand the different shadings that any given communicator might be using in their message. Like many things in our earthly life, this understanding comes from age, experience and good interaction skills. We can understand and empathise with a person's emotional state far easier if we have experienced something similar at some time in our own lives. When training younger mediums attending my seminars and development circles I always try to stress this point. The easy part of mediumship is making a link and receiving a message from the spirit world. For someone born with psychic abilities and skills, this spirit communication can be achieved through meditation, training and practice, but understanding the nuance of what a spirit is trying to say, and that it might be difficult for him or her to express exactly what they want to, is what makes someone a much better psychic medium. I've been able to hear messages from the other side for almost all of my life, but being able to pass on a communicator's sensibility and not just his or her words is what I try to learn and improve on every day.

In this particular case I began to sense that the grandfather and the first wife were not meant to be the main communicators. They were what I like to call 'enablers'. They were helping a shyer spirit to come forward and say what he had to say. I felt that the male spirit in question was testing the water, deciding whether to come through himself or not. I felt that this was the father of the lady in the audience.

'You know what I have to say is that your dad is in the background of all this. He's a bit shy about coming forward, which doesn't feel like his personality, so I sense that he has something he is unsure as to whether to say or not.'

I looked at the lady and saw the tension in her face. It was as if she was trying to will him to say what he had to say.

'He was a very odd man,' she said, sounding troubled.

'He's telling me that he's ashamed about not having settled the financial matter in an acceptable fashion before he passed away.'

The lady looked at me. 'So he should be. Thanks, Dad.'

I continued, 'He says that when you and the other person do your research into Vivien's side of the family you will understand more.' I felt the link starting to fade. 'I'm sorry about the monkeys!'

The lady stayed behind after the programme and agreed to be interviewed by the show's producer. Her name was Celia and she filled in many background elements to my reading. By all accounts her father was a very strange man. He came from France and his life had been marked by periods of great mystery. The standard family joke was that he had allegedly owned a pet monkey when he was younger, and he was always promising his children that he would take them to the zoo to see such a monkey, only he never did. That little anecdote kind of summed up the man, for it was only after his death that the family found out he had worked for the secret service as a spy. After moving to the UK for the latter part of his life he had had many complex business interests including a gentlemen's strip club. He had at least two wives (that were known about) and had left a complicated financial trail behind him. It was this part of the reading that had hit home the most. Apparently when he had passed away his will bequeathed his money to another person in the family and Celia's mother had been left with no financial security.

The producer asked Celia whether she forgave him. 'In all honesty I have to say that it's been such a long time I don't really know who he is. So it's a bit difficult to forgive him, since I don't know who "him" is.' Fair point. She was glad that he had come through feeling ashamed. Knowing this would at least make it easier for her to consider forgiving him, but she was waiting to take a trip to France with another family member, where she hoped that she would understand his life and personality a bit more as the story unfolded.

There are many families with secrets, some more potent than others. I want to share the following story with you because it is really quite sweet. In this case I was approached by a couple of spirits, one male and one female. I knew that they were not husband and wife. The lady was elderly and seemed as if butter wouldn't melt in her mouth. So you might say that I was totally unprepared when I was shown a bottle of Spanish fly. I apologised to my spirit couple, explaining that obviously I was mixing them up with another message, but they both looked at me sweetly and said that there was no mix-up. They were categorically showing me a form of aphrodisiac for increasing sexual potency!

Rather sheepishly I turned to the audience. 'Does anyone understand why a sweet old lady would want to speak to someone who had found a bottle of this substance?'

There was an understandable silence, punctuated by the odd nervous chuckle.

I explained that occasionally I get things that I'm not quite sure how I'm meant to interpret and tried to find another piece of information.

The couple said to me, 'Tell her she knows what we mean!'

A good medium has to be able to think extremely quickly. When messages from the spirit connect to you, they are often extremely fast, often very fleeting and you have to be able to latch on to them quickly. One of the things that you will often notice from mediums when they are working is that they become physically agitated, pace up and down and often talk a lot faster than they normally would do. This is because the body has to respond to the rapid changes and stimuli that are occurring in the mind. I also feel that they become more observant because of this heightened state of sensitivity.

'Tell her she knows what we mean!'

A lady put up her hand and said that she understood the message. I asked her where she had found the stuff, and she caused a huge ripple in the audience when she told me that she didn't find it – she sells it!

'These people,' I said, 'love you to bits. Not only that, but they are killing themselves laughing spirit-side. You thought it would make them angry, but it makes them laugh!'

The lady in the audience went bright red! 'It's true, I do always say that.'

It didn't surprise me when they put a new image in my head.

'Would you also understand the joke about a pack of playing cards with nudes on? You sell those as well, don't you?'

By now the audience was in hysterics. The couple coming through were lovely, sweet people. They didn't reveal the nature of their relationship to my lady in the audience, but they knew exactly whom they wanted to speak with.

'They're making jokes, but I feel there is something deeper, it's something you need to hear from them.'

I concentrated.

Then the male spirit told me to tell her the following. 'There is nothing you have ever done, and nothing you will ever do, that will make him ashamed of you. Whatever you have to do to get through life they will both never be ashamed of you.'

And with that my communication concluded.

The lady explained that the couple were her father and his mother. Her father had passed just before she was born and in later years she had taken care of his mother. She said that her 'nan' had passed recently and in the few months preceding had spoken of being with her son again.

She explained that she had grown up without too much money or schooling, but she had started a business from scratch selling lingerie and occasionally would have a laugh by going through some of the more risqué catalogues with her 'nan'. She was the only one of her crowd to start a business, and she had to fight quite hard to keep it going. She said, 'It's good to know that they are basically still laughing at me and what I ended up doing with my life. When I used to go round to my nan's with my catalogues, she used to have a good old giggle about them with me – that's what she was like.'

A few months before the reading, the lady had expanded her business and started selling 'adult novelties'. She had sent all her friends the 'nude playing cards' for Christmas. Of course what resonated most for her were the words they had used about 'never being ashamed of her'. When she started the new business she felt guilty at what she was doing and always used to ask her grandmother what her father would have thought and she had always told her that her dad would never be ashamed of her trying to stand on her own two feet. To hear this confirmed and how proud they both were of her was of great support and she told me that a weight had been lifted from her mind.

## I've been there too

I've had my fair share of family issues in my life. A decisive one was obviously when I 'came out'. I have to say that I've never found discussing my sexual orientation all that fascinating. I've never pretended to be anyone other than who I am, and my private life is just that, private. However, getting my family's support was vital to my ability to continue to function in my initial career in retail management and my subsequent one as a psychic medium. To this day not all my family are comfortable with it, but by renegotiating their and my expectations from our relationships (for example, that I cannot provide grandchildren) we have been able to continue to love and support each other.

A second more recent event was when my mother went into a coma in 2000. She was very ill, having already been poorly for a year. We were very concerned about her, she couldn't eat; she was losing massive amounts of weight and was getting very confused a lot of the time. We kept requesting more information from the doctors and they kept saying they couldn't find any obvious reason why she was losing weight. In June that year, in the early hours of the morning, I received a call telling me my mother was seriously ill and had been taken to hospital. At the time my brother and I hadn't spoken to one another for nearly two years, because of a big disagreement over another family matter. Consequently there was a great deal of tension between us.

I rushed to the hospital. My mother had gone into toxic shock; she was extremely ill and was on life support. The consultant said that there was little possibility of her pulling through. He asked for permission to turn off her life support machine. I argued with the consultant about turning the machine off, although it was difficult for me to explain that I was basing my decision on the readings that I was picking up around my mother's aura.

Luckily there was another consultant who decided that there could be no harm done in leaving the machine on for another couple of days. I spent all of Friday and Saturday with my mother just talking and saying, 'Mum if you need to go, fine, but if you can stay, stay because Dad really needs you.' On the Sunday afternoon I began to detect changes in the brightness of her aura and felt extremely confident that we had made the right decision about not switching off the machine. Thankfully she began to get better and her kidneys started functioning normally again. There was no question of doubt in my mind that she was going to recover. I was receiving direction from a spirit guide who was passing on messages to me about the state of her health. One doctor asked how I knew so much about the symptoms and I replied to him that I had a friend in a 'high' place.

Like so many before me it took this crisis to put certain things into focus. The sideshow to this illness was that our family had to pull together to deal with what was going on. Not only were my brother and I forced into close proximity, but we also had passionate and differing opinions regarding the condition and fate of our mother. Her illness put a few things into perspective and my brother and I talked over a host of issues. Our falling out had been based on a malicious lie spread by a third party and now he realised how untrue it had been. Although accepting of my gift he admitted he felt a little intimidated. However, this dramatic event made us realise that we had to mend our differences for the sake of our mum and dad. My brother and I had simply had to re-negotiate our relationship. We had to ask each other what we wanted out of it and work out what was truly important for us. We both realised that we were never going to agree on very much in life, but we are still flesh and blood and have to continually try to work towards as good a relationship as we can have.

For my part I had to be brutally honest with myself. I also had to see what behaviour my brother was letting me get away with. Had he taught me that it was OK to treat him in a certain way? The truth was that I could expect no more from our relationship than I was prepared to put in.

I suspect that most of us will be in some kind of stressful hospital situation at some point in our lives. I remember getting only about five or six hours' sleep in the two days I sat guard over my mother. One of the things I reflected on was that an essential part of the nature of the child-parent relationship is to perpetually ask ourselves whether we did the right thing. Even when we know we have, there is always a part of us that thinks we could have and should have done better.

For a lady called June it took a message from her mother to dispel her many fears about these kinds of feelings.

'I've got a lady that's been trying to connect to me saying she's called Martha and that she considered herself to be a "nice" lady.' I looked at June and asked her if she knew where I was going with this information.

'Martha was my mother,' she said. I could see that June was uncomfortable sitting with me. To be honest most people are not all that relaxed at the beginning of a reading, but June seemed especially tense.

I continued. 'She was being visited in the home three times a week.'

June nodded that yes she did visit her. 'You were never impressed at the overall cleanliness of the home, were you? It became very upsetting for you in those few weeks to see her becoming so frail. She knows that you tried to cover it up as much as you could, but she knows that you were in fact very, very upset.'

June continued to nod in agreement.

'She wants to thank you for trying to get her better care and attention. And she's saying that she's now aware she didn't like being dirty and unwashed.'

Suddenly I felt a sharp pain coursing through my right hand. 'How did she hurt her hand?'

June said, 'We never found out.'

'Poor love. Her hand was in such a state and she's just saying to me if only you knew the whole story.'

I tried to focus on the hand, but this gentle messenger wouldn't elaborate further. Instead she told me to tell June that, 'The truth is that it was painful, but by that time I had come to the point that it was time to go, and it wasn't important any more.'

I began to see a pastoral scene of water. It was a painting.

'Was Martha an artist?' I asked.

'No,' said June. 'I am.'

'I see a watercolour painting of a pond scene.'

June smiled. 'It was a winter scene – a frozen pond. I gave it to my mother and it was on her wall.'

Martha then asked me to mention a new name. 'Lucy or Lizzie?' June started to cry and I asked her if she wanted to carry on.

'Lucy is my daughter.'

'Where do I have to go with a connection to ovarian cancer?' The truth was that I already knew the answer. 'I think your mother wants you to know that she is with your daughter.'

June said that a wave of relief had spread over her.

'I also get the feeling of a family member that either studied calligraphy or copperplate or had beautiful handwriting?'

June smiled. 'My daughter had been learning how to do calligraphy, just before she died. We found all these pens that she had been using on her course.'

I could see a message being written before my eyes in beautiful handwriting. Slowly the words were revealed to me. 'You did what you did, Mum. You did what you believed you had to.'

I looked at June and said, 'They are fine now. They are both fine.' And that was the truth. I simply had an impression of the two of them happy to be sharing each other's company.

June explained further details after the reading. Her mother Martha had needed twenty-four-hour care in a special home but had not wanted to live there. Everybody at the home used to say what a 'nice' lady Martha was. June had always felt guilty that she had put her mother where she hadn't wanted to be despite the sound medical reasons for doing so. June had indeed regularly visited her mother three times a week, and had often felt the standards of cleanliness in the care home to be below what she would have wanted for her mother. However, they could not risk having her mother at home without permanent nursing staff.

One day she had visited her and found her hand bandaged. The nurse said they had just found her in the bed with blood all over the bedclothes and no-one ever found out what had really happened. Throughout the final few months of her mother's life June was always conflicted as to whether they had made the right decision. From a medical point of view they had, and yet her mother had been so miserable.

It was a relief to find out that her mother had in fact approved now that she was detached from the circumstances and could see things more clearly. June was also relieved to hear from her daughter, who had passed more recently from ovarian cancer. She had not expected her to come through as she had been strongly involved with the Church of England and didn't believe in anything connected with mediumship. I asked June if this was why she had looked so uneasy. June told me that the reason was that on the one hand she had been desperate to receive a communication from her mother and daughter and on the other she was terrified that both would use the opportunity to show their displeasure; her mother at the poor choice of nursing home and her daughter at the fact that June had gone to visit a medium.

All I could do was share with her my recent hospital experiences with my own mother and family. It seemed to me that June's behaviour had been exemplary. The time was one of great stress. She had liaised with other family members and those in the medical profession and then done what she thought had been for the best. The fact that she thought she could have done more for her mother was important. Not because it was correct, but because it showed the true extent of her love. We always feel we could have done more to help a loved one, but ultimately we have no idea what might have happened if things had gone the other way. We have to make the choices we think are for the best and then live with the knowledge that we tried to make the most accurate decisions under the circumstances.

The same applies to her seeing a medium. June could choose to believe me or not, but she had done what she felt needed to be done to improve her life. However much one loves one's family one cannot feel guilty about holding different views. I explained to her that the only way she could define herself as having a real relationship with her daughter was by both of them having slightly compromised their views. At least I was able to tell June that in my opinion her daughter still didn't agree too much with what I do!

## Moving on when it feels impossible

The key to getting on with family is to remember that we are all individuals with differences of opinion and we all have a right to those opinions. The temptation to ignore that opinion in favour of what you feel is best for another person whether it's your parent or your child will just create further tension. As I said earlier, parents do not own children; in fact nobody in a family owns anybody else. This may not be an easy concept – and I know won't be accepted in some cultures – but it does help us see the other person's point of view. It also touches on the all important question of trust. If we trust the other members in our family then we will listen to them and understand why they are doing what they do (provided it is not going to harm them or anybody else).

However, what happens when, despite everything, we can't get the love and support and forgiveness from our families that we need? What happens when we feel more isolated being part of family than alone? Should we persevere? And how should we feel about it?

You may have to step back and re-evaluate what family means to you. It may be that it is something you need to escape from if you are to find your own identity. This may not necessarily be because they are 'bad' people but perhaps they are simply unable to give you what you need. That certainly applies in cases where families do not show love. If you grow up in an environment where you do not feel loved and being within it makes you feel worse as the years go by, you may need to cut yourself off from that – not for good but for a period of time in which you can find the support you need to build your confidence and self-esteem.

The point is that you do not have to become like them. It's true that humans are very much programmed creatures and that most of our behaviour is learned from within family, e.g. cold people who can't show love will often come from families who behave in the same way. However, as many people have done, you can make the positive decision to break the chain of events and ensure that negative behaviour is not passed on to future generations. It will be tough but you do not have to perpetuate your family's bad experiences and attitudes, be they violence, aloofness, poverty, racial hatred, alcoholism etc. As Oprah Winfrey has memorably said, 'I don't think of myself as a poor deprived ghetto girl who made good. I think of myself as someone who from an early age knew I was responsible for myself, and I had to make good.'

In the introduction to this book I mentioned that sometimes we have to create our own 'family' due to distance. For example, someone may move to another city and their work will make it impossible to connect with their family often. They may be travelling overseas and leading a fragmented life. In these cases they will meet people in similar situations and, over time, will create their own 'family'. While they are not blood relatives, they will support and care for each other in a very loving and modern way. This principle can be applied to you if you decide that you have to disengage from your family in order to lead a more positive life. Remember, you are not doing anything wrong. You are just finding yourself. That is your right.

## A happy thought

I want to describe a certain phenomenon that happens to me sometimes. On occasion I can see the spirit of someone standing near to the person I am reading for. It doesn't always happen; mostly I see or sense this spirit in my head, but sometimes I can look out over an audience and detect a sort of human shadow that lingers next to someone.

On one particular occasion I was in the middle of a show and I was drawn to two ladies. One was obviously the daughter of the other, such was the close family resemblance. As I was reading for them and passing on messages from the spirit world, I could definitely sense the spirit of a man coming through, sitting between these two ladies.

I explained to them that sometimes a spirit wants to show that they still care and they try to protect their loved ones by placing their shadow imprint over a person, but in this case it was as if the man was sitting directly between them. He was not 'hovering' over them from behind, but was placed squarely in the middle of them. Not only that, but he was distinctly laughing at me for 'not getting it'. I told the ladies of my feelings and they too laughed. All I could say was that I knew he was between them at this very moment and that he thought it highly amusing that I could detect him without knowing exactly why.

After the demonstration the ladies came up to me and explained that the spirit was of their late husband/father. He had been cremated and instead of putting all the ashes into an urn they had used some of them to be made into a unique set of key rings! (A service I now gather that can be provided by certain funeral homes.) As they were coming to the demonstration they had both brought along these key rings and placed them in their pockets. During the reading these two key rings had been next to each other in their respective owners' pockets, meeting in the middle, directly between them!

Now I can't say that I'd recommend this course of action for everyone who wishes to memorialise a beloved family member, but what I can say is that if we do take responsibility for our family members then they will always stand beside us, both on this side of life and from the other side.

Family problems can be difficult to get a handle on as there might be a lot of people involved. Also most of us are not used to looking at our families objectively – we tend to think they are just our family and that is how it is. However, a bit of reflection and analysis along the lines I've described in this chapter can sometimes take the heat out of difficult situations.

## Strategies for coping with families

- To maintain a relationship both sides may need to compromise some of their beliefs. Be aware of other people's needs as well as your own; this way, your relationships have the best chance of growing and continuing.
- Even if something has 'happened' to you that you feel was not your fault, in order to improve your life it must become your responsibility to deal with the ownership of the problem. Work on the practical, not some ideal.
- Ask yourself if this person actually means a lot to you. If so then you must make the decision to put more time and effort into maintaining this relationship.
- When planning to speak to the other person, think of a time and space where you can talk about your relationship calmly. Try to solve the problem before the day is through.
- If you are in a situation where a relationship has turned particularly sour and you are being hurt or abused by someone, it may be best to end or change the relationship.
- The more contact you have with someone the more you will need to compromise.
- It is wrong to think that we can become great fonts of limitless love for some family members. We are sometimes just too different and we may need to accept those differences and carry on at a distance.

# 4.

# Connecting: being part of the world

*'No man is an island, entire of itself.'*

**JOHN DONNE**

A life without friends is soulless and empty. Friends don't just give to us; they allow *us* to give, which in turn makes us feel more positive about the world and ourselves. Friendships are based on a completely different set of rules than those of close family (e.g. parents or children). Because we choose our friends we have to put the time in to make the relationship work. With friends we are more aware of the need to share and exchange, whereas with family things can often be one-sided. We will tell our close friends things that our families may never know. By doing so we are able to make sense of our life experiences and are better able to figure out where our place is in the world.

## Do you know who your friends are?

Obviously you have many acquaintances in your life, but who are your true friends? When I was at school I can remember one teacher asking us this important question. Of course we all replied that we had loads of friends (certainly more than a sad middle-aged teacher!) He asked us if we were sure. 'Imagine you were stuck in a city away from home with no money, and it was pouring with rain,' he said, 'and then you phoned around to ask who would leave that instant and come and get you. Now how many friends do you have?' The point was well made. A good friend is not just a fair-weather friend: they are there through thick and thin. So it is time to add having good friends to our list of things that can add more meaning to our lives and widen our appreciation of the world. Yet sometimes you might not know when someone is your friend.

'Cheltenham Ladies' College? Are you sure? OK then, I'll tell her!' I was being directed to a rather well-to-do lady in her late fifties in the audience.

'I'm speaking with the spirit of a lady who was together with you many years ago at school.'

'Are you sure?' asked the lady. 'I don't recall keeping in contact with anyone from my schooldays.'

'She's telling me her name is Jean and that she only went to that school for a couple of years. She says that you were particularly kind to her during her short time there.'

Jean said, 'I had many friends, but you looked after me.'

'Goodness, I do remember a girl called Jean but she wasn't

there for long,' said the lady with surprise in her voice. 'We wondered what had happened to her, but nobody ever mentioned her after she left.'

Apparently Jean had left the college suddenly and had not remained in contact. The spirit told me that she had been taken out by her parents due to suddenly being diagnosed with cancer and needing intensive treatment. For whatever reason, a decision was taken not to tell the other girls. Jean had passed over a few years later.

'She just wants you to know that she appreciated it,' and with that my communication ended.

It's funny but it's often simple messages like these that seem most to annoy those sceptical about the work of mediums. Frequently a spirit just wants to let a friend or family member know that they are well. And that's pretty much it. The trouble is that those who are sceptical seem to think the spirit should know all about the lives of those who are living in the physical world. My response is that spirit communication is like any other form of relationship between two communicators.

Imagine that you meet someone whom you've not seen for a while. You have a bit of a chat, ask how the husband/wife/children are and then move on. You are not expected to know what their living room looks like, nor are you likely to ask about it. Most spirit communications are simple messages of this type. However, that doesn't make them insignificant. Even a simple message of thanks such as the one expressed by Jean shows how even the briefest meeting can leave an impression.

The most powerful thing about this particular reading was not the message itself, but the effect it had on the woman in the audience. She certainly had never thought about Jean after leaving college and had never given this relationship another thought until I'd brought it up, but she now realised that she would re-assess all her friendships as a result. The idea that the way you relate to someone through the power of your friendship can affect him or her beyond his or her earthly life is a very powerful one.

Friendship is a two-way street. It is vital to our lives to have and maintain good friendships because of the positive effects this will have on us. To keep these relationships going and benefit from them we have to learn to become more attentive, more giving and more kind and considerate. Ultimately friendship will make us less selfish, which means we will be living our lives on a higher level. I think the next story demonstrates the level of unselfishness that we should all aspire to.

I started the reading with my communicator asking for his 'bro'. Now I like to think that I'm in touch with the younger generation and the way they speak, but the thought did cross my mind that if the whole reading was in street slang it might be a long afternoon!

I was drawn to a muscular chap with a shaven head, sitting with people I assumed were members of his family.

'I have someone here who is calling you "bro". I know it can mean brother, but I know it can mean friend as well – I know this guy was your friend and this is what he used to call you.'

The young man (who we later found out was called Pete) nodded and smiled in acknowledgement.

This is always the trickiest part of a spirit communication – I know that I'm on the right track, but need to provide some concrete information for the audience. I increased my concentration and tried to tune out any thoughts that might interfere with my communication.

'He tells me that you are still wearing the article that was his. In fact you've worn it every day since he died.'

Pete smiled and said, 'Yeah,' but I saw that he was still reluctant to fully believe what was happening. He wasn't going to get too involved ... yet. Many people don't get too excited straight away: they just want to wait and see.

The message continued. 'I'm glad I'm not throwing up all the time. At least that bit is a relief!'

Suddenly I could hear the Queen song *We Are The Champions* very clearly. 'He's telling me that he's still the champion of the world!'

For the first time Pete laughed. 'I can't believe he's still winding me up about it – even from over there!'

Now I couldn't stop. 'He's asking me to include the people sitting next to you in this conversation. He wants you to know that he's still glad you were the first person he told.'

Although he was what you'd call a blokey sort of guy, Pete wiped away a tear as I heard the audience go, 'Ohhh.'

I sensed a very private conversation that had taken place between these two special friends.

'He wants to thank you for helping him realise that it wasn't a shameful thing. You could explain it to his parents better than he could. He thanks you for explaining to them what he couldn't explain himself.'

Once I had passed on this information I felt a release of tension in the air and this gentle spirit went on to remember various evenings out, particular drinking sessions and even to chastise his mother for thinking she wanted to be with him when she had other family to look after.

'I told her not to worry about me all the time.'

As usual the story behind the reading is far more inspiring

than any of my abilities to deliver the message. Pete had lost his best friend Duncan to a rare virus that attacked his lungs and that was what had caused him to throw up all the time. Duncan had tried to remain as dignified as possible as his condition worsened.

'He was absolutely incredible,' said Pete. 'I don't know how he did it,' he added, the tears welling up in his eyes.

After he died, Duncan's girlfriend gave Pete an item of his jewellery, which he continued to wear every day as a memorial to his friend. They had called each other 'bro' as a term of affection.

Pete was still close to Duncan's family, which was why they had come to the demonstration together. Duncan's parents were very open-minded about psychic mediumship, but interestingly Pete was not so convinced. He had come to the demonstration in order to give them moral support. He seemed a really nice guy.

Like many close friends, Pete and Duncan affectionately made fun of each other: in this case it often revolved around the subject of football. Duncan was a Manchester United supporter and always teased Pete by saying, 'We are the champions of the world.'

Pete summed up their bond of friendship when he said to me, 'I'd pour my heart out to him and he would listen to me no matter what. He never ever thought any less of me no matter what I told him.'

When Duncan told Pete of his illness he needed a special kind of support. Not that his family were not supportive, but it was almost as if he needed someone his own age to say, 'It's OK, mate, I'm here.'

As Pete said, 'It touched me a lot, when he told me about

it. It's not easy to tell your best friend that you are really ill and there's a good chance you're going to die within a couple of years. To be honest, I didn't believe him, even right until the end when he was ill and in hospital. He was a fighter and he fought all the way to the end.'

It was only when I was watching these 'reveals' later on the television show that I understood what their special friendship had been about. Both Pete and Duncan's parents were interviewed by the producers. When asked what they thought of the whole experience, Pete (who, to be fair, was still trying to decide whether he fully believed in spirit communication) replied that it was irrelevant what he thought, he was just happy for Duncan's parents who were 'believers' and deserved to hear from their son as a reward for their devoted care for him. When they were interviewed separately, Duncan's parents selflessly explained how, unlike some of their son's other 'friends', Pete had continued to stay in contact with them and check up on them even after their son's passing. They said that although glad to hear from their son, it was far more important for them that his good friend Pete had been the main focus for most of the message. I came away thinking what an unselfish group of people they were. No wonder they had stuck together.

## Your differences can bring you closer

Making friends is easier for some people than for others. That's not necessarily because these people are cleverer or funnier than others but because they are able to tolerate differences in others. Often people will describe a friend as being 'exactly the same as me' but in truth some of the most rewarding friendships are where you are both completely different yet have an understanding of each other. As I write this I cannot help but think of my good friend Mark. We have known each other since we were four years old and have been popping into one another's life ever since then. We have stuck by each other through thick and thin, not because of what we have in common (he is neither gay, nor does he have much time for spiritualism and mediumship) but because we know that we will be there for each other.

Mark was actually the first person in my home town I spoke to about being gay and I can still remember his response of, 'So what? What's the big deal? Tell me something I didn't know.'

We would go around together to both gay and straight clubs, and he would suffer the sneers of many people for hanging around with me, but Mark was confident enough in himself to say, 'You think what you like. He's my mate!' To have someone who both understands you and is then willing to back you up is a blessing. A few years ago when Mark was between jobs he became a driver for me. Apart from helping him out practically, there was a sense of relief on my part that I could talk about my feelings in a much freer way than if I was being driven by a random company driver. A good friend is like a bullet proof vest, a protective shell that can ward off some of the ammunition that life throws at us.

There is no doubt in my mind that much of my own personal success is indebted to friends and in particular to John Austin, George Cranley and the other members of my development circles. Because of them I progressed from being a fairly mediocre, church medium into a professional medium who could go out and conduct séances and give demonstrations to thousands. Because of such people I was able to develop confidence in my gifts and be strong enough to go out and demonstrate to the world. All of those in the development circle were gifted in their own way and yet they were all prepared to focus on my skills and help develop them. For that I shall always remain extremely grateful.

From a psychic perspective it is interesting to observe how very good friends (examples also include married couples and long-time partners) are able to get so emotionally close to each other's way of thinking that they are often able to anticipate each other's thoughts. They're the people you'll find saying the same thing at the same time, being able to finish off the other's sentences, or even instinctively knowing when the other is about to call them on the telephone.

I would say that the link to these phenomena is ESP (Extra Sensory Perception), which can also be referred to as the 'sixth sense'. Out of all the different kinds of psychic phenomena, ESP is probably the most accepted by the mainstream. I suppose you can look at it as 'any sensory information that an individual receives which comes from beyond the ordinary five senses (i.e. seeing, hearing, smelling, tasting, and touching).' This perception seems to provide the individual with information of the present, past, and future and appears to be generated from another reality than the one our five main senses operate in.

ESP has been talked about for over 150 years and has attracted much attention and enthusiasm. Among the more common ways of testing for ESP is to find out whether or not one person can guess what is in another person's mind a greater number of times than would be expected by chance. The accepted methodology for this is the use of *Zener* cards. A pack consists of twenty-five cards, containing five designs – a circle, a square, a cross, a set of wavy lines and a star. I'm sure many of you have seen these icons without realising what they are

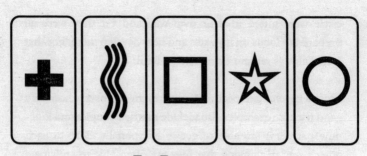

**THE ZENER CARDS**

used for. They were actually featured in the movie *Ghostbusters*. However, they are explained in many sites on the internet.

The simple idea is that one person looks at one of these cards while another tries to guess which card it is. The average result is of course a one-in-five chance. The question is, can someone with an extra sense improve on those results? Some experimenters have found they can predict higher scores for particular groups (for example, those who are interested and relaxed), and lower scores for other groups (those who show fear, negativity, or boredom).

There is, however, a real feeling that ESP does exist, only that it cannot be explained by physical laws. The scientific argument is whether the mind (i.e. consciousness) and the brain are as one or separate. When I give seminars I always like to point out that ESP is independent of such factors as location, time, age, intellectual ability or education level. It also seems to be able to function independently of the other five senses. It is as if it is a super sense, which is connected separately to the human nervous system. It does seem incredible that so many ordinary people can report a form of ESP activity happening to them at some time in their lives, often during a crisis such as an accident or the death of a loved one. Maybe it is the shock to the system that enables these messages to penetrate our consciousness more easily. However we choose to explain it, there does seem to be a unique connection between friends that operates on a very deep level indeed. The closer we get to true selflessness with our friends and family the deeper our perceptions and understanding of the other people seem to go.

## When friendships are in trouble

It is interesting to think that while our workplace relationships are governed by a set of rules, both formal and informal, our friendships rely on us doing things instinctively. For example, once a friendship has been established for some time it is natural to assume that you can make certain demands of each other and be assured of a response. A good friend is someone who accommodates your faults and vice versa. They need to put as much into the relationship as you do. I don't mean tit for tat, but you both have to make the effort. You need to be there for each other. You must have a sense of mutuality – you will both give each other practical assistance and emotional support, along with the enjoyment of each other's company. Within the boundaries of each friendship is a private relationship that is inaccessible to others. Friends have a history and an understanding of their connection to each other that separates theirs from all of their other relationships. At the basis of this is trust, the loss of which can be extremely damaging to a friendship. A friendship is a two-way thing, and if one of the parties has lost interest in the friendship, then it is important to realise either that he/she needs space and a little time, or that not all friendships are destined to work out. Having said that, you do owe it to your friendship to sort out why things are not enjoyable for you any more. Don't give up on someone too easily when after all, there must have been a reason you were friends in the first place. I always say please try to sort it out now. Don't wait until they have passed on to wonder what might have been.

## Expanding your circle

In writing this section of the book there were several topics I wanted to tackle. One in particular was the idea of community. I don't want to go on about the supposed decline of British society but it's pretty clear that we don't engage with our local communities in the same way we did thirty years ago. So many times have I sat there biting my lip after a reading, comforting a grieving person and thinking to myself, 'Where the hell were your friends and neighbours in the aftermath of this bereavement and your loss? Why were you so alone?' Even worse are those stories you see not infrequently in the papers about people who died alone and whose bodies were not found for days or even weeks. That just should not happen. It's more than tragic, it's utterly disgusting and it makes my heart ache for those people.

But what exactly is a 'community'? There are obviously many definitions, but I take the following approach: the idea that community is about bonding with the people around you so that you are part of each other's wider lives. Community in this sense can refer to relations among nations, among people who share some interest or among the residents of a neighbourhood within a larger settlement. For me one of the most important roles of community is as a network of people all giving each other help and support. Being part of a community allows a person to have a 'cushion' in knowing that, through good times and bad, there will be people to share it with and support them if necessary. A community where people depend on each other is a good thing in a society where, increasingly, many of us live alone, away from our families. The obvious and more traditional examples of communities are those based around religions. These provide their own culture and beliefs for understanding life, often built around physical structures – a temple, mosque or church – to pray in, meet in, educate in and centre the community around. They also provide teachings through all phases of our lives and of course that all-important practical support in troubled times.

Personally I feel most closely attached to the Spiritualist movement, whose views I find myself most strongly identifying with. However, I definitely feel that religious communities of all kinds can be beneficial as long as they aim to contribute to the overall quality of life of their members and work with the wider community, not against it. If you are not part of or interested in joining a religious community (and to be honest even if you are part of one) I still think belonging to other 'mutual interest groups' can be a really good thing. I'm talking about anything from following the local football team to joining a book club, drama group or delivering for the local 'meals on wheels'. By attending meetings you will discover you have the potential to meet many new friends, discover a new side to yourself and give to others. As I said earlier, friends help us to extend ourselves and to experience more and a community is a good way of opening up your mind and your life. Community is like family to those who have none (or are not in contact with them) and a wonderful addition to life for those who do. We often forget that one of our responsibilities on this earth is to help others and make the earth a happier place. Our modern society tends to make heroes out of those who seek fame and celebrity, but the real 'supermen' are those who voluntarily build and sustain communities. They don't make the headlines but they do make a difference to people's lives.

I'd like to share with you an experience about the value of community. I was recording an episode of *6ixth Sense* and was being drawn to an unassuming chap at the back of the studio. I began to feel an elderly lady coming through who felt a great deal of affection for this man.

I looked over at the man in the audience and asked him if he had a grandmother in spirit.

He did one of those double takes that people often do when I question them and then said, 'Yes, I do.' I automatically assumed that my communicator was that relative.

'She's asking me to thank you for all the lifts,' I explained.

The man looked disappointed. 'My grandmother died long before I could drive,' he said. I could see the faces of people in the audience drop in dismay.

I asked my spirit for confirmation, and she definitely was showing me a car and some leather driving gloves. I thought that maybe the message was for another member of the audience, but I was brought back towards the same man.

I asked the spirit to move aside and continued with what I thought was going to be my next communicator.

This time the spirit of an elderly gentleman came through. He too wanted to speak to the same man.

I knew I was on the right track here, yet was missing a vital component. I turned to the man. 'You also have a grandfather in spirit.'

'Yes, I do,' he said. I wasn't sure if I was getting somewhere.

My communicator then showed me the same leather gloves I'd seen a few moments ago.

'Maybe it was your grandfather that you used to drive around?' I asked.

The man shook his head.' I have no idea why my grandfather wants to talk about my driving. It doesn't make any sense to me.'

I was beginning to feel odd. I knew what I was sensing, knew I had been drawn to the correct audience member, but either he or I was missing a vital piece of information. Sometimes it can be like that and you have to persevere a bit in order to put the jigsaw together.

I tried to make another contact. It was the spirit of a different elderly lady. I scanned the room to see where I was being drawn to, only to find myself back at the same man I'd started with!

When I asked what message she wished to pass on, she replied, 'I just wanted to thank the gentleman for always stopping next to the kerb!'

And then a floodgate opened in my mind and there were several spirits all jostling and all wishing to say, 'Thanks for the lifts!' It was rather jolly really, having all these spirits saying thank you at once!

I realised that I'd been incorrect about the man's grandparents, but I insisted that all these nice old folk were coming through for him, and this set of messages he accepted with pleasure. The obvious conclusion was that he was a professional bus driver, but I sensed on a psychic level that this was not correct.

After describing a few of the old people and their eccentricities and foibles my communication ended. It had been an overwhelming outpouring of love and appreciation from many different communicators, all commenting on small but thoughtful things such as his sweetness, patience and willingness to do the odd favour or fix something about the house.

The man was greatly amused by all this and told me that for a few years he had been a volunteer for the local old age centre. 'When I had time off work I used to take some of the local old people to and from their homes or to the local community centre. If they needed it, I'd help them with their shopping. It was great to see their reaction when I popped into their houses just to see how they were. They were always so happy to see me; it made my day.'

All I could say to him was that most people have friends and family who watch on from the spirit world. In addition to that this man had a whole community of senior citizens watching over him! Wouldn't it be great if we all did? But he had earned it. He had made an effort to reach out to others, had expected nothing, yet now he was getting back all this appreciation in return.

## Friendships are good for our health

As psychologists will tell you, when people do not have enough contact with others they become selfish and even worse can end up despairing and depressed. Friends are vital in life (especially for those without close family) because without them we would be lost, rather like someone who is lost in a city where they don't understand the language. Friends help us make sense of life. They are there for us when we have nowhere else to go and no-one else to talk to. They will come and go throughout our lives. But if we make it a priority then there are some friends whom we have for life and who will always be there for us.

## Joining a community

- You have to think outside the box. The people in your community will not be identical to you, but they will share common beliefs or love for a particular subject. Examples of communities include those based around religion, hobbies, sports, children, gender or age.

- Turn off your television set (unless it's *6ixth Sense* or *Psychic Private Eyes*!) Honestly, watch less TV and communicate with real people instead. You cannot be part of a community on your own. Your DVD collection is comforting, but a poor substitute for real friends.

- If it is hard to get out, find ways of staying in contact with others via the telephone or on the internet.

- Start to talk to your neighbours. Cook extra food and share what you have. Give each other a night off from the kitchen each week by inviting them in to finish up the weekend leftovers. Take this to its logical conclusion and organise a street party.

- Buy things in local shops. Engage with the shopkeepers and their regular customers. Read the local newspaper (often free) to see what is going on.

- If you have children or a pet, then take them to the park. Actually speak to the other parents or pet owners.

- Support your local neighbourhood school, library or town hall. Get involved with their activities. If you've got a skill and/or some spare time, offer it. Very few organisations do not need volunteers!

- Not involved with a group that shares your hobby? Then set one up! Now is the time to create a 'Classic Car club', 'Loch Ness monster appreciation society' or 'Obscure pop group fan club' etc.

They'll be honest with us like no-one else can, and will provide assistance and feedback when needed. They will provide companionship and together we will help each other enjoy new experiences and appreciate life more fully. The real friendships we establish will enrich our life and open up new possibilities. Like all things in life, having true friends is not something that we can take for granted, nor are they owed to us by life. We have to work on making friendships, then nurturing them, and never fall into the trap of thinking that they can be abused without any negative effect.

## Some friendly thoughts

- Friends choose each other. It is this voluntary aspect of friendship that is regarded as the wonderful part of the relationship.
- While most people enjoy meeting new people, those they have known over time sustain them more. The continuity of relationships over the years is an important source of security, comfort and self-worth.
- Real friends are there for you through thick and thin. They do not disappear when the going gets tough.
- The ability to make friends is often based on a person's ability to tolerate differences rather than look for things in common. It is these differences that increase our appreciation of each other and the world.
- The key to maintaining friendships with other people is to understand that everyone has their faults. Anyone who thinks they are faultless is unlikely to give enough to the relationship. If something goes wrong, ask yourself why before blaming the other person.
- Look at your wider community as a source of contact and friendships. Reach out to others and they will be there for you.

# 5.

# Forgiving: leaving the past behind

*'Forgiveness is the attribute of the strong. The weak cannot forgive.'*

**MAHATMA GANDHI**

Have you ever watched a dog with a bone? Have you noticed how it will hang on to that bone with grim determination for ages? No matter what you do, it refuses to part with it or let you near it. That is of course natural behaviour for a dog. That behaviour won't cause it any harm and will probably amuse its owners. For a human, however, hanging on to negative feelings like a dog with a bone is neither a good idea nor a healthy one. Letting go of feelings is absolutely vital to our well-being. By that I don't just mean expressing your feelings; I mean being able to let go of the negative or angry ones you have in order to forgive somebody.

For some people forgiveness comes easy while others struggle with it. Often a person's excuse for not forgiving another is, 'I want to make them suffer.' But who is really suffering here? Is it you or them? By persisting in hanging on to those negative feelings about a person or event you are only making yourself feel worse. Do it for long enough and you'll find yourself locked into a time and place that you can't leave. That sounds like a waste of a life to me. You need to learn to forgive not to give the other person peace, but in order to find it yourself.

## It is not up to us to spread hurt

Sometimes people can hurt us so badly that we want them to suffer in the same way we have done. But what we should realise is that whether they show it or not, that person is suffering because of who they are and their behaviour. At some point in their life – or afterwards – they will see that they have behaved in an intolerable way and they will go through all sorts of regret. And if they continue to behave badly towards others, they will eventually get it coming back to them. It is not up to us to carry the burden. Our task is to find the best way of moving ahead with our lives. That may not mean forgiving them in a real sense, but it may mean learning to dismiss them from our thoughts in a calm rather than vengeful way.

I would say that a fair proportion of people who attend my readings have themselves been damaged by events or other people. Either they are looking for forgiveness or they are waiting for somebody to say 'sorry'. Unfortunately it doesn't always happen in the way they want it to.

I was passing on a message to a man called Gerry. Forty minutes earlier we'd commenced a one-to-one private sitting.

I passed on my initial thoughts.

'I have a woman here with me, who calls you "Ger", and who gives me a motherly sensation. She isn't showing me much at the moment, and the thing that strikes me here is the silence. She's not telling me anything either. I think that she used to like sitting in her chair and watching the world go by rather than commentating on it.'

Gerry was not a happy man.

'But why didn't she say sorry? How hard would it have been to say sorry, once she'd come through anyway?' He shook his head and looked down at the table.

The truth was that I felt the reading wasn't going all that well. It happens sometimes. Sure, I had a link with this woman; however, as the saying goes, 'the silence was deafening'. As you will have gathered from this book, most of my communicators are not stuck for words, but here was someone who was making me aware of her presence and the person she wanted contact with, but not of any message to pass on. I tried to persuade her to give me some information that would at least validate her message in Gerry's eyes.

'She asks me to tell you to pass on her love to "P".' Gerry nodded, showing that he would, but, looking into his eyes, I could see that he was desperately pleading with me for more information.

I reached out for more evidence. I sensed a game of tennis being played out in front of me.

'She liked tennis, I gather.'

'Yes,' he replied impatiently.

'*More. Please show me more*,' I was asking. 'When you were little, Gerry, you used to dress up with "P". You used to pretend to be cowboys and Indians. You were always the cowboy. No matter how hard "P" tried you were always the one who wore the star – the sheriff's badge.'

Gerry started to cry. Many people cry when I read for them, but usually I know what has caused it. For the life of me I couldn't work out which piece of this story was so emotional for him.

'Please just go on,' he said, trying to bring himself under control.

'Would you understand why I am being shown a guide to the flowers of the British Isles?' I asked. 'She is showing me lots of flowers and I can see them next to their names in Latin.'

'She knew all the flowers,' he said, looking up for the first time. 'That was her special thing. We could be on holiday anywhere and she would tell us the names of the flowers.'

By now I knew that there was something of great importance that she wanted to say, but something was holding her back. I tried to coax her gently, yet ultimately I failed.

'As she fades she's just asking me to tell you to stick with the painting; watercolours in particular.'

I told Gerry as gently as I could that the link had been broken. I knew from his initial reaction that this would not be a good idea but I had no choice. His emotional upset had been replaced by a great deal of anger which he was having difficulty controlling. I asked him about the painting and he said words to the effect of, 'What's the bloody use? It was all accurate, the cowboys, the flowers, my watercolours, but what was the point? She still can't say sorry to us!' His whole body was now trembling with frustration and anger.

I asked him if he would mind sharing his story with me. If I couldn't help him as a psychic medium, then maybe I could as a counsellor. Some years ago I did a bereavement course with the Samaritans and I have found it very useful in these situations.

'I knew it was my mother's spirit. I and my brother (the "P" in the message) had a great childhood and she was very good to us. One day, after displaying various symptoms for a while, she was diagnosed with early-onset senile dementia. But she didn't tell us. She just killed herself.'

'So you and "P" are naturally feeling hard done by,' I said softly. 'She left you without any explanation or saying goodbye.'

'I just can't forgive her!' he shouted. He slumped in his chair and spoke quietly. 'Why should I? She hurt me. Us.'

I explained that spirits are not always ready to pass on the messages that are specifically needed, and that if the person was not such a good communicator on this side of life, they do not suddenly change their personalities on passing to the next. In this particular case I felt that his mother still had to come to terms with what she had done. In the same way that she had been unable to express her feelings before her tragic act, she still could not do so, even now from the spirit world. Ultimately I had no idea why his mother never said 'sorry' (and I would never lie by pretending that she did), but what I did know from the little I had seen of Gerry was that his guilt and anger over what had happened and his inability to forgive his mother for what she had done were slowly destroying his life. We talked for a long time after the reading and I'd like to share some thoughts from that episode.

Unfortunately, I'm sure that, like Gerry, many people reading this book will feel that there is someone in their life whom they have no desire to forgive. A random list of events I've come across that cause such feelings includes: being betrayed by a loved one, being let down by a friend, suffering physical or mental abuse, being bullied at work, resentment at someone having committed suicide, suffering a physical injury or financial loss ... I could go on.

The refusal to forgive someone for what they have done is often made worse by confused feelings of guilt and anger. People can often think that maybe they brought it upon themselves in some way, or feel extreme rage that they did not act differently or make different decisions under the initial circumstances. All this resentment and anger ends up taking control of a person's life. It gets into your brain and manipulates you until it seeps into every aspect of your daily routines and ultimately poisons you and others around you. Remember what we said in a previous chapter about 'being what we think'. If every second of our lives is consumed by thoughts of anger and revenge we will become cynical and nasty about everyone and everything in our world. The result is that we lose all our abilities to find love and spirituality.

There are good reasons for people like Gerry to feel wounded and to retain their anger and resentment. Ultimately it is the result of a lack of closure on the treatment they received at the hands of another, who never said sorry or asked for forgiveness. Yet what I tried to explain to him was that he still needed to forgive the person who had wronged him. By this I meant that he did not have to forget what had happened or say that it was fine but it did mean giving up the emotions that were ruining his life. The question was not whether his mother deserved forgiveness, but whether Gerry did.

I explained to him that in an ideal world she would have said sorry, but she didn't. Rather than wait for her to do so, he had to act as if she had, and make a decision that from that day on it was he who controlled his life and he was not going to let those bad feelings ruin it for him. When a person has been wounded, feelings of anger over their grievances are not in themselves something evil. Yes, it's absolutely normal to respond emotionally to what is happening at a particular moment; however anger is supposed to be a fleeting emotion – just one of many – not something that we dwell on without end. The only thing worse than being hurt is to carry that hurt and keep it alive within you for ever. It should not be allowed to burn brightly. If it does it will burn out everything that is good within you.

As most therapists and psychologists today try to help people 'learn to forgive', the idea is that forgiveness is something you learn to do, not something that is within you. I believe it is indeed something we have to learn to do if we wish to live our lives in a more productive and peaceful way. I believe that it is an honourable skill for us to learn, as we are the only creature on this earth with the capacity for such action. If a gazelle escapes from a lion that was trying to kill it, both animals carry on their respective roles of prey and predator a day later. Only human beings can wound each other emotionally as well as physically and have the ability, and need, to find forgiveness.

I stood before a small group of about sixty people in Peterborough at a demonstration that had been organised by a local spiritualist group. As I scanned the room I knew almost immediately where I needed to be. I looked at two women sitting in the audience. They were obviously mother and daughter.

'Almost as soon as I started this session,' I said, 'I could see a young lad in front of me taking me over towards the two of you.'

They looked at each other and then back at me as if to say, 'Yes, go on.'

'I have to be honest and upfront with you. I have a boy here who says that he needs to speak with you, but he wants to make sure that you want to hear from him.'

The daughter, who I found out later was called Sandra, said yes almost immediately. Her mother hesitated. I waited for her to tell me what she wanted me to do. After a few more moments of hesitation, during which she looked around the studio, she looked at me, cleared her throat and said, 'Yes, I do, Colin.'

'He says he should have taken better care of himself and listened to his mother, but he was led astray by others.'

I suddenly felt a cold chill go up and down the back of my spine. I rapidly became aware of exactly how he had passed from this world. I took a breath as I continued. 'I don't want to upset you but I must be straight here and say that this fellow is telling me that he was murdered.'

I waited to see if there would be any adverse reaction. The daughter was nervously fidgeting with her handbag while her mother held her arm. 'Please carry on,' said the mother, and her daughter nodded in agreement.

I closed my eyes to try and feel out more information. All of a sudden I felt as if someone had punched me in the stomach several times and then in the neck, and I saw this chap lying in a pool of blood. The vision in my mind was so clear that I could feel the warm blood gushing down my neck into the base of my spine.

I explained my interpretation to the two women. 'I feel that he was stabbed several times, but the fatal blow was one to the neck.'

At this point the mother's stiff upper lip finally cracked and she began to cry. Her daughter, Sandra, seemed a lot more together. 'Can you tell me more, please, Colin?' she asked in a very strong, clear voice.

The boy started to show me a pond full of ducks. I could hear their quacking as if I myself was standing next to a park pond. I told them what I was sensing.

Sandra's mother smiled. 'When he was young, I'd take all the children to feed the ducks. He loved coming with me and he was so funny when he tried to imitate them.'

'The feeling that he's giving me is that they could not stop the bleeding. An artery, a vein is cut or severed and they could not stop the bleeding and he literally bled to death.'

I could see the inside of an ambulance. 'Was he attended by an ambulance crew?'

Sandra wrung her hands and took a deep breath. 'They called an ambulance for him but he died on the way to hospital from massive blood loss.'

'Were there two inquests?' I asked. 'He's showing me the number two.'

Sandra said, 'There was supposed to be a second one but it never happened. There should have been another one.' Her voice trembled.

Sandra's mother looked straight at me and asked, 'Who did it?'

I let my mind relax as best it could under the circumstances and tried to focus. It can be very pressured for a medium in such situations. You're trying to concentrate on the communicator; meanwhile the people are anxious for immediate news.

'All he is showing me is a group. It looks like a gang fight that got out of control.'

'But which one was it?' the mother asked. Obviously he had been in a number of fights.

'It is too hard to tell,' I said. 'I sense a lot of fighting, and then it all seems to get out of control.'

The mother seemed to lose interest after this part. Sandra however was more receptive and nodded at me to continue.

'He wants you to remember him as a nice boy. The moment of madness wasn't really him.'

'I know.'

He started to tell me that he had a brother, and asked them to send him his love. 'Tell him he's too clever to follow in my footsteps.'

I sensed that the reading was drawing to a close, partly because I always get more tired when I feel the effects of violence.

'He's asking me to tell you, his mother, something – "You have to forgive, Mother," he says. "Never forget, but you have to forgive."'

As I looked into her eyes I cannot say she was convinced. After a short break and a few more readings I managed to have a word with the two women. Sandra's brother had had an uneventful childhood, until a couple of years previously when he got involved with a new crowd of friends. His mother did not approve of them and had tried desperately to prevent him from associating with them. One night he and some friends got into a scuffle outside a nightclub with another local gang. Knives were drawn and despite the fact that no-one probably intended to murder anyone, the son was fatally stabbed. As is often the case with gang fights, no-one was charged with murder because the police had no idea who had administered the fatal blow. The fact that there was no one specific person to blame seemed to make the family's grief worse.

I thought about this particular reading long and hard as I got ready to go home. I knew that the mother did not want to hear this message asking her to forgive. I knew she was too distressed and upset to want to have anything to do with the murder of her beloved son. On one level I completely understood that. Yet I also understand exactly what her son had meant for her to do in his message.

## Forgiveness is helping you, not them

For some people the barrier to forgiving is that the moment has gone and often the people have too. They may be dead, in jail or simply have moved away, making it more awkward to get in touch with them. Not only have they ruined your life, but it seems they are controlling you from where you cannot reach them. In this case Sandra's mother had no-one asking for forgiveness from her so she had made the decision – consciously or otherwise – not to forgive.

Meanwhile her son was trying to tell her that you do not need the permission of the one who has hurt you to move on. That doesn't mean you should overlook or excuse their behaviour. By releasing the resentment and hatred you feel towards them you unburden yourself, not them. What she had to do was free herself from the pain of her injury, not free the injurer from what he did.

Forgiveness is not surrender, but quite the opposite. It is a conscious decision to regain control of your life from the person who caused you the pain. By hanging on to the pain of the boys who killed her son, the mother had made an emotional bond with those people for herself. When we blame someone else for our suffering, when we believe that they are the cause of our pain, then we need 'something' from that other person in order to feel better. If that 'something' is not forthcoming then we carry on the blame and resentment until it is. Forgiving and letting go allows us to stop waiting and concentrate on the processes of healing rather than hurting.

I strongly believe in the powers of psychic mediumship to help people heal and find forgiveness and meaning in their lives. However, as a medium I must always be sensitive to a person's feelings. It is not my place to tell you what you should do if you have been given a message. I may have a fair idea of what I think you should be doing as a result of a message from somebody who has passed over, but please don't expect me to suggest it. My view is that if you have asked for a reading or have been in the audience when a message has been communicated to you, it is up to you what you do with it. I know there are some mediums who believe that they must pass on every scrap of information they receive regardless of the effect it might have. I have to disagree with this approach and say that those who trained me taught me that a responsible medium is one who sometimes has to make the decision not to pass on a certain piece of information. Sometimes one has to realise that not only will nothing be gained by the recipient receiving all the information, but in fact it might cause more difficulties and more heartache. Sometimes I just know that the message in my head is for a particular person in the audience, but they will not connect with it. I have to always be aware that however accurate I might be, I might be reminding a person of memories that they have no wish to revisit. Sometimes a person might appreciate a message but does not want to receive it in front of other people.

In my role as a medium I am very careful not to raise people's expectations too high. There are many people who attend my shows who expect that what will be heard will be all positive and happy. It won't. There are times when it will be very shocking and I am careful in how I deliver those messages. Let me give you an example. A gentleman connected to me, wanting to speak to his two sons and his daughter in the audience. The message for the two sons I was happy to pass on; however, the message to the daughter I couldn't pass on: he was effectively apologising for abusing her as a child. I just wanted to hug this woman, but as for saying anything to her in public, forget it! I felt I had no right to go into the details of what he was saying sorry for, nor get involved in whether his actions merited understanding or condemnation on her part. All I said was, 'Your dad would just like to say sorry.' I have had many tough calls like that.

Forgiveness allows you to imagine a better future, one that is based on the possibility that your hurt will not be the final word on the matter. It challenges you to give up your destructive thoughts about the situation and to believe in the possibility that the future will be more than simply dwelling on the memories of past wounds. You do not need to forgive for their sake, but for yours. You also do not need the other person present to achieve this. They don't need to know, don't need to say sorry, don't need to change their ways *because this is about you*! Forgiving helps you, not them, carry on and regain your life. That doesn't mean you accept the hurtful things that people have done to you. It doesn't mean you are best friends or even like them. It means you like yourself. By forgiving you are being kind to yourself; making sure that your anger does not take up time or space it does not deserve. Finally it's up to you whether you choose to remain a victim or become a survivor. What are you going to do? Let go of the pain and move on? Or hold on to the pain and become a victim? It's your choice.

## Reflections on forgiveness

- All of us, at some point in our lives, have been hurt and wounded by the actions or words of another. If you focus continual attention on this pain and hurt, it starts to become a habit, and like all habits it can be hard to break.

- No matter what you feel someone has done you must learn to let go. If you don't then your life will be destroyed by the bitterness and anger as it colours everything else in your world.

- Forgiving someone does not mean absolving them of their responsibility for what happened. It means letting go of the pain and hurt you feel in your heart and reclaiming control over your life. You should not forgive as a gift to the person who has wronged you; instead you are doing it as a gift for yourself.

- It is important to stress here that there is a difference between forgiving and forgetting. One can forgive, without forgetting what happened. You may *never* forget, but you can *choose* to forgive.

- In an ideal world the person who wronged you would come to you and ask forgiveness, but you must accept the fact that some people will never do that. That is their choice; they did what they did and must live with the consequences. You can only control your behaviour, not theirs.

- Healing the hurt in one's life takes time – sometimes a very long time. Forgiveness means you spend the rest of your time dealing with your healing and not with your hurt.

# 6.

# Searching:
# the quest for
# spirituality

*'Religion is not identical with spirituality;
rather religion is the form spirituality
takes in civilisation.'*

**WILLIAM IRWIN THOMPSON**

Many people in parts of the West today are not connected to,
or brought up with, religious beliefs. Even so, that doesn't stop
an increasing number of us searching for meaning in our daily
lives, something that is not necessarily religious but *spiritual*.

At some point we have all asked ourselves:

• Is there something out there?
• Is there more to life than we understand?

- Is there something or someone or some energy looking over us?
- Does our spirit live on somehow after we die?

Most of us are not asking for a lot; we just want something that will bring us peace and some sense of meaning in this mad, chaotic world. Is that too much to ask? I don't think so.

## Why are we looking?

I think that one reason why we are hearing and reading much more about people's search for spirituality and meaning is that we live in an age where we have many possessions but they're not making us happy. Even if you're not the richest person in the world, you are still likely to have a house full of things, many of which are truly not necessary to your life. Through my work I've also found there are a few more reasons why people start searching.

1) **Personal tragedy:** If you have had your life disrupted by tragedy or trauma you may want to find a way to restore order. The most obvious examples are the ill health or death of a friend or loved one or your own serious illness.

2) **Wars and disasters:** Just the knowledge of wars and natural disasters like the Asian tsunami can make a person feel that their own life is out of control. You don't even need to be close to it to feel concerned. After such a momentous event, people will often embark on a search that may sometimes cause them to rethink their lives.

3) **Emotion and desire:** The most obvious example would be falling in love, or the desire to find true love.

Many of us speak not just of finding a partner but a soul mate who is at one with us in spirit.

We still haven't answered the question of what spirituality is. How will you know when you find it? There are so many different attempts to define what spirituality is or what it can do for us. Some of the ones I like are:

- It is a general sense of peace and connectedness to others as well as to ourselves.
- It is a source of strength in the presence of distress.
- It is at the heart of our well-being.
- It is an integral component of healing.
- It enriches all aspects of our physical, mental, emotional and community life.
- It is expressed in the attitudes, beliefs, and practices that influence people's lives.
- It enables us to experience the transcendent or higher power.
- It embraces fullness, meaning, love and hope in the journey of life.
- It is a life force that promotes hope, encourages healing, and helps us to embrace others and ourselves.

Please don't think these are set in stone – they are just my own thoughts to start you thinking about spirituality. I remember one reading that certainly gave me a lot to think about in terms of what spirituality could be.

On this occasion I was having difficulty working out what the feelings I was being given meant. I gathered that this man wanted to re-connect with his large family but I also knew they were scattered and not all in the audience. Sometimes it's difficult to figure out the best way to do something but you just have to start.

'I'm looking for someone who comes from a big family but is alone here today.'

While I was saying this I was also trying to block out all disturbances so I could focus on a name.

'I have a person here giving me the name of Liam who has passed to the spirit and the circumstances aren't quite explained.'

'Yes. I think it's for me,' said an older lady, slowly putting up her hand.

'Are you sure you can accept the name Liam and you come from a large family?'

She nodded silently in agreement.

'All right, my love. The feeling he's putting into my mind is that this message is for the family and in particular one lady who is this side of life and it's so important he gets this message across to her because she's stopped believing.'

'He's right,' said the lady quietly. I think she felt a bit unsure as to whether she should acknowledge such a fact.

'She's completely lost her faith,' said Liam. He suddenly became very clear. 'She thinks that there is no God, because she can't understand how He would let this happen.'

'Yes,' the lady said, still a bit hesitant. 'The woman is my mother.'

Liam came through with very specific instructions. 'Can you tell Mum to open the drawer up, get it out, hold it in her hand again and get her faith back?' It was a strange message but the lady seemed to understand.

'Yes,' she said, starting to sound a bit more positive in her responses.

I could hear nothing for a few moments. I knew this spirit was still with me, but he was taking his time and putting his thoughts in order. This is not uncommon.

He was back. 'Tell her I know they visit my grave twice a year. I want them to stop it because it's pointless.' He continued, 'All it keeps doing is reminding everyone that my life on earth was tragically cut short, and it serves no purpose.'

'But what do we do now?' said the lady, sounding lost and helpless.

Again this young man's spirit took his time.

'You won't find the answers at my grave. Or in James's truck. You need to look within your faith. I love you and Mother, but you must keep believing.'

I knew that this lady wanted to hear more even before she asked, but that was the end of my communication. Liam was no longer linked in to me.

The lady's name was Siân and she explained that she came from a large family of ten boys and Liam was one of her brothers. He had passed away in his early thirties as the result of a car accident. Her partner was the James in question, who drove a truck and often used to take Liam out with him on long journeys.

Her voice trembled as she told me more. 'After his death the family stopped going to church and my mother in particular lost her faith in God. We started going to visit his grave regularly and looking after it.'

Siân had had an argument with her mother over a picture of Liam that her mother talked to every day. The picture had been removed from a living-room wall and placed in a bedside cabinet drawer along with some personal objects.

When asked about the message Siân seemed strangely

relieved. 'We knew it was doing us no good to brood at his graveside, but it had become like an addiction. We were almost too scared to stop going so we just kept doing it.' I sensed that she was pleased that Liam had said what he did. Still she was understandably sad and confused.

Both mother and daughter had considered themselves deeply religious but now felt let down by Liam's tragic death.

For me this message gave a lot of food for thought. Siân and her mother, blinded by the terrible grief and pain of their loss, had given up believing in anything and were simply damaging their own lives. I think they had looked at religion in the wrong way. Being religious is a way of life, not a guarantee of life. Belonging to a religious or spiritual group, no matter what you believe in, gives you the support of a group and can really help you during times such as bereavement. Liam's message to them was pretty clear. By cutting themselves off from their faith they were suffering. To find the answers they were looking for they needed to re-connect to their religious traditions and spirituality, not run away from them.

'I found the reading very spiritual,' Siân told me later.

'Why?' I asked, wondering what had made her use that particular word.

'It made me more sensitive to the *essence* of my life,' she replied.

I think that all of us, like Siân, are trying to find this *essence*. We are all trying to make sense of our everyday life experiences and find some purpose in our existence. I'm not afraid to admit that I'm still learning and trying to grow every day as I look for my own essence.

But where do you look? That is the big question. For some people the search becomes a lifetime quest as they travel the world trying different religions to see which one might fit. Well I think they may as well be looking under the sofa because I don't think you really have to go far to find it. Also, I don't think you can buy spirituality like a souvenir! And you know what? You can have spirituality without religion. Just because you follow a religion or belong to a church it does not necessarily mean you are living a spiritual life.

Immediately I can hear some of you asking, 'Are you knocking religion, Colin?'

I most certainly am not. I realise that many people believe that religion has been responsible for endless wars and much human suffering. However, I think it's important to point out that there is a difference between the religion itself and the people who might use it to further their own ends. In other words there is a big difference between religion and the religious! As it happens, I do admire people who follow a religion and make its practices part of their daily lives. Practices and customs are an important comfort in life and can often provide optimism and hope for the human spirit. In short, religion is sometimes, but not always, the road to spirituality.

One of the many questions people ask about mediums is whether they belong to any of the main established faiths or religions. Some do but others like me are affiliated to the Spiritualist movement in the UK. Spiritualism is the belief that the human personality survives death and can communicate with the living through a sensitive medium. For me Spiritualism gives the definite answer to the question, 'What happens after I die?' I accept that for some people this is just not a question while for others it is much more; it's a conflict.

There was a man who came to see me three times in all. Each time he came I could see nuns and priests around him but I just couldn't find it in myself to tell him. On the third occasion he came, I saw a vision of a papal ring.

'I'm sorry,' I said. 'I really have to verify something that's been bothering me. Do you have some sort of connection with the Catholic Church?'

'Yes,' he said, 'I do.'

It turned out that he was very senior in the Catholic Church. When he came to see me he wore a very plain suit. He explained that he needed to come and see me because he was struggling with what I did and his religious beliefs.

'My Catholic teachings tell me I shouldn't be here but I feel there is something I need to find out.'

Each time he came we would talk for two hours or so and this was no different. He then said that he would like me to read two books of his, books about the teachings of the Catholic Church.

'I'd be happy to,' I replied, 'if you take some of mine and read them.' I loaned him two books of teachings by the spirit guide Silver Birch, and we agreed to read them and meet up in a couple of weeks. The appointed time came to meet.

'There is nothing I have read in your books that I could contradict or disagree with in any way whatsoever,' he said. 'Yet my religion tells me that the way spirits come forward is forbidden.'

I reminded him that I was a Spiritualist, not a Christian, and asked, 'Is it not correct that the vast majority of teachings in your books have been communicated through people called prophets? Why is that different?'

'This is my dilemma,' he replied.

115

## Finding spirituality amidst the noise

My own career path has also given me something to think about in terms of how I try to define a personal sense of spiritual satisfaction from my work. One thing I have found is that there is a real connection between feelings of uplifting spirituality and intimacy. There is definitely something special about one-to-one readings, but of course these days I mostly appear in front of large audiences. So how does that feel spiritual?

Certainly there are certain issues that all mediums have to deal with when making the transition from giving small local demonstrations to performing in large theatre or television shows. As I started to become one of the better-known mediums in the UK I went up and down the country taking my mediumship to different demonstrations in Spiritualist churches. On the one hand I was considered to be a fresh face, and on the other there were those who were thinking, 'Who is this young upstart?' There was definitely an element within British Spiritualism that would have liked to keep it as a private members' club. You had to be invited, and then nominated by two people – it used to be like joining a secret society. They felt that any invasion of this club would somehow make it less spiritual. I remember going along to a Spiritualist church in East London one night and there was an old lady who was the honorary president there and she said, 'How many people do you think are going to come tonight?' and I said, 'Oh, probably a hundred to a hundred and fifty–' and she looked at me down her glasses and her nose and she said, 'We have never had a hundred and fifty people here.' The poor love nearly had a heart attack when over 200 people turned up that night. You sensed that it didn't feel right to her; it wasn't 'spiritual'.

My own view is that these criticisms are balanced by the fact that we are reaching a larger audience. Because of this, there is a wider interest and more people are encouraged to look deeper into the world of the spirit. On the other hand, many people definitely come to the demonstrations simply to be entertained, and I would really be a liar if I said I did not enjoy demonstrating my mediumship on a big stage in front of thousands of people. However, I treat my work professionally and while I don't mind being entertaining when presenting my mediumship, mediumship in itself is not just entertainment.

It's very hard to maintain an intimate atmosphere in a TV studio or theatre so, to try and not lose it completely, I make a point of staying behind to talk to people after my demonstrations. I obviously cannot provide messages for everyone, but meeting people is a constant reminder of what it is I'm expected to do with my life and to appreciate the gifts I have been blessed with. These meetings often provide me with many spiritually uplifting moments, which remain with me.

Among the most enthusiastic people in the audience are many who never get a message; they just come for the joy of watching other people receive spirit communication. I think in a way it gives me a great sense of faith in human nature, because these people come along (obviously there is some part of them that hopes to get a message) and take so much pleasure out of others getting what they want. To see this constant kindness in people uplifts me.

Another example is the knowledge that even people who do not receive messages can often have their faith strengthened. Many people come up after the demonstrations and say things like, 'I've not had a personal message, but I've seen you do it for other people and this has restored my faith in the fact that there *is* something after death.'

There is an enormous pleasure in seeing people go away from demonstrations who have been moved in some way. I would not be human if I did not get some sense of fulfilment out of that. Whenever I am worn out or feel that it has all become too much, it is these people who remind me that being a medium is my life and I have to carry on, for all the detractors and all the people who question the validity of what it is we do.

Perhaps then this is the message for all of us, even if we cannot define spirituality exactly – if we help another human being become spiritually uplifted they simply take us with them and we too feel great spiritual fulfilment in our lives.

## Spirituality shifts and changes

Often when I'm in a particular building, I will feel the spirits of those who were connected to it in some way. For example, reading once in a fire station I felt the spirits of several firemen who had died on duty. The place where this happens to me the most is in the theatre. (I don't know if this is connected to the outgoing personalities of most of the people who work in the entertainment business, or because I spend too much of my time giving demonstrations in theatres!)

On one particular occasion I was contacted by a very lively spirit, who told me that not only had she loved the movies, but also that she had known or had met some famous movie stars.

'I think you might be talking about my mother,' said a slightly trembling voice from the audience. The woman put up her hand and asked me if there was further information. What other information might I give her?

'She's telling me that she loved watching the old movies, and if she saw them with you she'd explain to you about all the people in them, and tell you what she knew about them.'

'My mother was on the stage as a young lady,' said the woman. I later found out her name was Patricia.

'Did she have dealings with movie stars?' I felt this was a crucial piece of information that had to be verified.

'Of course,' said Patricia, not a little proudly. 'The ones who also appeared on stage with her.'

'Did your mother know Margaret Lockwood?'

'It's funny you should say that,' she said. 'She always talked about her as if she had!'

I continued, 'Through no fault of her own, your mother became a little bit sharp in her last years. I think she had always been a fiery character, but I think she became a little bit spiteful.'

Patricia nodded thoughtfully.

'She wishes to say sorry and hopes you understand that she was really at the point where she couldn't control and understand exactly what she was doing.' I felt that I was reaching the main crux of the message. 'Do you remember a beautiful brooch that your mother used to have; it was rather large, with diamonds and gemstones in it?'

Patricia said, 'Yes I do.' She seemed excited.

I continued, 'Well she's rather sad that it's gone to a place where it's never worn for fear of being lost or broken. She really does wish that she had said it would come to you.'

I knew that I had to phrase the next bit delicately for fear of hurting Patricia's feelings. 'She really became rather bitter towards you at the end of her life and she did take some actions that were meant to spite you. She's very, very sorry for that.'

'I understand,' said Patricia. She was not excited now.

I could see this piece of jewellery very clearly in my mind. 'Your mother says that if I could ever get to hold the brooch I would be able to use my psychic knowledge to explain more about the circumstances.'

'Unfortunately that is unlikely to happen because I don't have it.'

'The last thing she asked me to tell you is she's glad you cut your hair! She knows you'll understand. All I can add is that your mother is back to the lady she once was, and not the very bitter one she became. She wants you to remember this: "Nothing goes missing, it just changes form."'

After the demonstration I had a long chat with Patricia. She knew it was her mother from the references to old movie stars. Her mother and her aunts had all been on the stage and the theatre was in their blood.

'My mother had an amazing life. She toured all over Europe with many famous stars and she used to sit us down when she was at home and tell us stories about them!' Often she would take her children to the movies and delight in explaining who the stars were.

Patricia continued. Her voice was full of emotion. 'Towards the end of her life she developed Alzheimer's. She didn't remember much of course but she seemed to clearly remember her experiences on the stage.'

The brooch in question was a particular favourite of Patricia's; she identified it completely with her mother. It brought back many happy memories of growing up with her mother's love and those times when they sat around hearing her stories.

Suddenly she sat up very straight and seemed almost businesslike. 'Why did you want to see the brooch?' she asked me.

I began to explain to her that there is a fascinating use for crystals in the world of the paranormal and that is something called *scrying*. A crystal lobe is used to put the clairvoyant into a state of hypnosis so that they can attempt to see visions in the crystal. The reflection of light in the crystal forms *repeat points* for such hallucinations. These images are often symbolic and are either disconnected and vague or very clear. What makes scrying so special is that the person doing it has no control over what they see and the images can be based on the past, present or future.

I had of course seen this piece of jewellery very closely in my mind's eye, but had also wanted to hold it and see what would happen with my spirit connection. I suspect that with Patricia and her mother's emotional attachment to the piece it would have produced some interesting results had I attempted to scry with it.

Patricia nodded thoughtfully. 'I would have loved to know what you could do but that's all in the past now.' Unfortunately, because her mother was suffering from Alzheimer's disease she had acted out of spite and confusion and given the brooch to Patricia's sister, who had never worn it since.

I asked her what she thought her mother had meant when she said, 'Nothing goes missing, it just changes form.'

Patricia laughed. 'I think it's obvious,' she said.

I asked her to explain because, although I understood, I wanted to hear her say it.

Like many people, when she first started to care for her mother it had felt like a spiritual experience. She was doing what was right by looking after the person who had given her life, but as the years went by she had become emotionally tired and worn out.

'After my mother passed on, I felt desperately lost and spent a lot of time searching for something. I had no direction and had no idea where to find it. I was bitter about the brooch because it never meant anything to my sister but then I learned that I had to look beyond that.'

As time went by Patricia had learnt to cope, understood that her mother's behaviour was caused by her illness and found new goals to strive to achieve. Initially her loss of the brooch and her mother had symbolised a loss of spiritual meaning in her life.

'The truth is that the meaning in my life had not disappeared; it had just changed form. I don't think spirituality stands still.'

I think this applies to so many things in our lives. The search goes on, but as we get older and accumulate more experience, the answers take on a different form. Ultimately your spirituality is yours so it must mean something to you. It might come from your religion or it might come from the feeling of contentment you have when you do something nice for somebody. It might be the few moments you take in the day to think about the positive things in your life and remove the negative. Do you see what I'm saying? The important thing is that it means something to you. That is what makes it spiritual.

## Some thoughts on spirituality

- Spirituality is our attempt to make some sense of the world around us. It is a search that often begins when we are dissatisfied, discontented or distressed with some element in our lives.
- Spirituality can have many definitions and many forms but in the end it is fundamentally about a search for inner peace, happiness, contentment and hope.
- You may not have to search far and wide for it; it could be right in front of you. While religion can help some people find their spirituality, it is also possible to develop your spirituality without having a religion.
- We can use our spirituality to make others feel better and in doing so enrich our own lives.
- Spirituality can change forms throughout your life, but it will still be there if you want it to be. You just have to keep your eyes open.
- Spirituality is a very personal thing. You don't get it from another. You find it within yourself and when you do it is yours to keep.

# 7.

# Accepting: coping with death

*'Think not disdainfully of death, but look on it with favour; for even death is one of the things that nature wills.'*

**MARCUS AURELIUS ANTONINUS**

Let's face it. The British and Western cultures generally don't do death very well.     Death is perhaps the most difficult of life's events to cope with, yet one that we take very little time to prepare for. In addition we tend to see death as something unfair. Death is the ultimate robber because it takes away the things we value most. Even more unfairly it may take them away far too early and when we least expect it. And quite often all we can say is, 'Why?'

There are no lessons in school or university on how to cope

with the feelings that everyone will experience through these losses. We should definitely spend time preparing for death and learning to face it. It is important that we do become more familiar with death and learn to accept it as a normal occurrence. If we manage to include death as one of our discussion topics then, while we will still feel loss and sadness when it happens, we will be better equipped to deal with those feelings. We all fear death but, if we fear it so much we refuse to consider it, then we will be hurting ourselves even more. Allowing that fear to take over will deprive us of the opportunity to say goodbye in the best way we can. The result is that many of us will never achieve the closure we so badly need. To give you just one statistic from a website, apparently there are over 500,000 deaths each year in Britain. Not all die peacefully and 'naturally'. Not all have time to say goodbye. However, about 25 per cent of those people will die at the end of a long illness, which means there is time for us to get that closure. Yet most of us have no idea how to achieve it.

## You are not the only one feeling useless

I think a lot of people are simply not sure what to do when they find out that one of their loved ones is dying. Rest assured that this is completely normal, especially given that we spend most of our lives not discussing death. If we discussed it as much as we discuss sex, for example, then I think we would be more comfortable. From my own experiences I am aware that many people want to know more.

'Are you that guy from the TV?'

'Well, I'm *a* guy from the TV,' I replied, getting into the taxi.

'It's you. The one who speaks to dead people, like that kid in the Bruce Willis movie!'

I wondered what direction this conversation was heading in.

'We were talking about you in the pub the other day. My missus loves your show – every bloomin' day she watches it.'

'Have you ever seen it?' I asked tentatively.

'Oh yes. I've seen a few of them. Don't take this the wrong way,' he replied, 'but I think it's all a load of rubbish.'

Actually I didn't take it the wrong way at all. The truth is that I was quite chuffed. People from all walks of life are now discussing in pubs whether there can be life after death because of shows like *6ixth Sense*.

I did ask the driver why he thought it was rubbish though and he said, 'I just don't think you really can speak to the dead.'

'So why do you watch?' I enquired.

He hesitated for a moment. 'This might sound a bit weird,' he replied, 'but I like it when people have a bit of a cry. They seem to end the show much happier than when they start!' He paused then continued, 'Sometimes it makes me think of my old man who died a few years ago. You can't speak to him, can you?'

I explained that I wasn't picking anything up. The conversation stopped after he mentioned his father.

The taxi driver, while not totally convinced about what I did in my work, was curious. The personal evidence I have suggests there are a lot of people out there who have experienced death and who want to know more in some way. Rather than discussing it on a personal level, they have found other ways to do so. Just look at how it was discussed after the tragic death of Diana, Princess of Wales. I honestly feel that was a key moment when people in this country started to talk about death and grieving. In some ways I think it allowed a lot of people who would not normally show emotion to reflect on their own experiences. Hundreds of articles were written and the mass media showed the collective grief of all the people queuing to pay their last respects and lay floral tributes. After that you saw an immense increase in the popularity of shows like *6ixth Sense*. The viewing figures for that show were very high and it ran for an amazing 150 episodes! In addition, for the last three years I have demonstrated in front of at least 200,000 people each year.

This connection between the popularity of mediums and times of tragedy such as the death of Diana is nothing new. If we take a look at the history of modern Spiritualism, then we can see that the popularity of mediums increases in times of crisis. Spiritualism and the work of mediums were increasingly sought during and after the First and Second World Wars. In my own work I have seen a significant rise in clients or people trying to meet with me after the Falklands and (first) Gulf War. The reason for this is simple: during times of crisis people see others dying and tend to think a lot more about their own mortality. It is perfectly normal.

## How are we supposed to react?

To understand how we are to deal with death, we need first to think about how the dying might feel. Dr Elisabeth Kübler-Ross was an eminent psychiatrist who devoted her life to death and the dying, generating much valuable debate and discussion along the way. Through her strong commitment to the subject, she did much to de-mystify dying and to draw attention to the treatment of the terminally ill. Kübler-Ross identified five stages in which the dying comprehend what is happening to them. They are:

1) **Denial and Isolation:** 'This is not happening to me.'
2) **Anger:** 'How dare God do this to me!'
3) **Bargaining:** 'Just let me live to see my son graduate.'
4) **Depression:** 'I can't bear to face going through this, putting my family through this.'
5) **Acceptance:** 'I'm ready; I don't want to struggle any more.'

The list has been both praised and criticised by grief experts. Some say the stages are useful in getting people to express their emotions; others say the stages are too rigid. In any case I think it gives us an idea of what a person must go through. The question is, how do we, the living, approach the subject? It's not my place to give you any hard and fast rules about when to talk about dying. It's a very individual and highly personal thing. However, I would say that you need to do it at some point. Some people are quite willing to talk about it early on. Others prefer not to do so until the very end, when they realise their illness is not going to be cured. The truth is that most people who are dying know that they're dying. One reason they might not want to discuss it – aside from their own fear of the unknown – is that they think they are protecting the living. What can you do? Much of this will be about your preparedness to listen and to try and identify which stage the person is at. If they are in denial, then it is not a good time to try to have a discussion. Much of the time your role will be to be there to listen. They may not say very much but it is important to them – and you – that their isolation is not made worse. The hardest thing as a human being is to do nothing, but sometimes that is what you must do. Of course if they want to discuss it, the boot may be on the other foot: they may be one of those people who is so open about their death they even plan their own funeral. This can seem bizarre to the living but it is very healthy and positive.

At the end of my shows I sometimes invite questions from the audience, and often I'm asked why some spirits come through soon after they have passed, while others often wait for years before they communicate with their loved ones. I always answer by saying that different people have different attitudes to death in their lifetimes – those that are attuned to it and can confront it find it easier to adapt to the spirit world than those that never wanted to think about it.

One of my most moving readings ever involved Stephan, who wanted to hear from his wife who had passed a few months before. She came through to me with a clarity that I wish I could experience with all my readings and thanked her husband for all the funeral arrangements, including the special items he had placed in the coffin. It was these items that convinced a sceptical Stephan that I was indeed communicating with his late wife, for there was no-one else who knew what he had put in the coffin.

Afterwards I asked Stephan what had happened and he told me his wife had fought a short, courageous battle with cancer, but had died much quicker than the doctors had anticipated. I told him that she knew what was happening but hadn't wanted to worry him or their daughter. I knew this not through any psychic means but from the way she was in the spirit world. She had adapted so quickly because she knew that her physical time on this earth was ending and it was time for her spirit to move on.

## Grief is your healing process

When someone close to us dies, we tend to avoid the brutal reality of the event with positives such as, 'God doesn't give you more than you can bear … s/he is in heaven now … they'd want you to be strong, not cry … just think of the good things about their life.' That is all well and good, but it's just not grieving. The only way to grieve well is to, well, grieve. Grief is as individual as a fingerprint; however, the need to do so is universal. Some people do all their grieving at the funeral. Others grieve for much longer. You need to develop some sort of ritual for yourself that gives you some peace and sanity in all this because apart from anything else, you will feel lost. Perhaps when you're feeling like this you may decide to go to a place that you both enjoyed and just sit silently and reflect. You may decide that you'll do this as your private ritual and you may do it indefinitely. There is nothing wrong with that. As well as thinking about the person who has passed, it'll give you time to take stock of your life. Everyone needs such a time and place. Unfortunately, grieving has a beginning but no middle and end. So it won't neatly organise itself to finish and it won't be consistent. Sometimes you will feel angry at the person who has gone or even at God – whoever your God is. Sometimes you will feel regret at the things that were not said. But that is OK. This is your time to feel that.

There are no rules for how long 'normal' grief lasts, since it varies by individual, type of loss, and relationship to the deceased, but studies have shown that it takes the average person six months to a year before they really start to come to terms with their loss. First of all we have to be patient. We must acknowledge that it is normal to suffer pain after a severe loss. We have to be strictly honest with ourselves. When we say we

## Reasons for not resolving our grief and moving on

- We might have suffered the loss of a loved one in a way that was traumatic, stigmatised, or unexpected.
- We might have been present when a death occurred and not used to seeing such things.
- We might have suffered more than one lost loved one in a brief period of time.
- We might have had parents who were unable to grieve normally, and were unable to be good role models. If these and other adults did not talk to us as children after a loss and explain what was going on, or left us with the message that one should, '*grieve alone*' or '*not talk about it*' then we can find ourselves unable to express ourselves properly when we face the loss of a loved one.
- We might not have known about certain issues related to the health of our loved one that might have prolonged that person's life.
- We might not know the exact cause and circumstances of a loved one's passing.
- We may have been judged negatively in the past (or seen it happen to others) for our grieving patterns. People often say things like '*snap out of it*' or '*get on with your life*'. Society frequently pushes the message that one must keep a '*stiff upper lip*' and not grieve.

are grieving for a lost loved one, what we really mean is that we are grieving for ourselves. We are thinking thoughts such as, 'How will I live without them?' or 'How can I live on my own?'

These thoughts are completely natural and intrinsic to our ability to heal ourselves.

We do however need to learn how to communicate with them and then say goodbye to the relationship that has ended. Unresolved grief is almost always about undelivered communications of an emotional nature. There are a whole host of feelings that may be attached to those unsaid things. We do not need to categorise, analyse, or explain those feelings. No-one is saying one shouldn't feel these things. All these feelings and fears are not illogical or irrational. They represent a normal, healthy range of emotions about painful loss combined with our society's limited ability to talk openly and honestly about grief.

## Helping others overcome grief

How can we help minimise grief for those who are mourning the loss of a loved one? Grievers seem to be walking through quicksand, yet they usually have a heightened awareness of what is going on around them. In particular, they are very aware of being judged, evaluated, or criticised. An unhelpful comment runs the risk of making matters much worse. My experience of bereavement both personally and professionally suggests that the most important thing is not to do or say anything that might cause someone to bottle up their feelings. There is no point in repeating mantras such as '*Time heals all wounds*' or '*The main thing is to keep yourself busy*' when they blatantly do not work for all people and might even damage a person's feelings. Most importantly, though, they inhibit people from talking about 'what happened'. Most people who have suffered a loss want and need to talk about 'what happened' and talk about their relationship with the person who has died. This does not mean that every griever will want to have a detailed conversation with everyone they meet. Nor does it mean that you always have to make yourself available to someone who may need more time than you have. What I suggest is that instead of avoiding the subject of the loss, or reciting a mean-ingless phrase like '*It was for the best*', you at least acknowledge a person's bereavement. A simple comment like, 'I was sorry to hear about your loss,' can be very helpful to a griever who may be questioning his or her own sanity because the world no longer makes as much sense. A person's feelings and emotions need to be heard. They do not need to be fixed or placed under headings. The best help we can give someone is to give them the confidence to talk about what they are feeling. No-one should be afraid of expressing their sad feelings and no-one should be deprived of talking about the treasure trove of memories attached to their relationships with people who have passed over.

## Death hurts me too

People often assume that because I spend all day dealing with the spirit world I must have no fear of death and no real empathy for those who have lost a loved one. Other people have said to me that they think a medium is incapable of understand-ing a 'normal' person who has lost a loved one and is unable to just contact their spirit whenever they like. There are even those who think that my fellow mediums and I are actually taking advantage of those who have lost a loved one and are cynically exploiting their grief. Obviously, I believe the opposite to be true; I genuinely feel that I have been blessed with a unique gift that must not be wasted, and should be used to bring as much comfort to those who need it as possible. But how does being a medium affect the way I think about death and the process of grieving?

Let me clarify another obvious point. A medium is first and foremost a human being who experiences life, love and loss just like anybody else. We are just as affected by the loss of someone we love. It is possible that I have a slightly different perspective when someone I know passes over, but believe me when I say that their absence hurts me the same as anyone else reading this book who has suffered a loss. I have shed as many tears over those who have passed over as the next person and will continue to do so as I get older and encounter more personal bereavement. What is correct to say, though, is that I do not fear death. I know that a person's spirit survives beyond the physical death of their body. However, just because I am not afraid of death does not mean that I do not value my life here on earth. The simple truth is that, like most people, I have no desire to die soon as there are too many things I would still like to achieve in my life!

## The nature of the spirit

When the physical body dies, a person's spirit continues as an integral part of the spirit world that exists, but in a different dimension to our world. Spirits are the same personalities and often choose to convey their messages by reminiscing about their characters or characteristics rather than delivering a speech on the meaning of life. Believe me, if they didn't show the inclination to do it while they were on this earth, they won't do when they have passed over!

Having said all this, I remember reading for a lady called Janine at a show in Cardiff. The weather had been particularly bad that afternoon and now an amazing lightning storm was taking place. On the way to the theatre I remember my driver remarking to me that it was going to be a spooky night. The weather made the theatre look like a set from *The Addams Family*. The air felt highly charged in a way I had never experienced before. Facing the audience I was more nervous than normal, and after a couple of genteel readings where spirits just wanted to come through and pass on their love, I was suddenly aware of a white-haired old man in a study full of books. The books lined the walls from floor to ceiling and the man was standing on a ladder that moved round the whole room, attached to a wall rail on wheels. On an old wooden desk in front of him various potions bubbled in small glass containers sitting on Bunsen burners.

'I know who that is,' piped up a woman in the audience. 'It's my father.'

'He's trying to tell me something about the nature and meaning of life. There is a bubbling test tube.'

The woman, whose name was Janine, laughed and said, 'Well, that's no surprise.' She seemed very happy. I felt a bit awkward because it was a very strange message but the main thing was that Janine was getting something that mattered to her.

As is my way, we met up after the show. Janine explained that she had been dragged along by a friend who was a believer in the spirit world. 'I feel silly admitting this but I came along for a bit of a laugh really.'

'That's fine, Janine,' I replied. 'You wouldn't be the first!'

Janine told me that her father had been an associate of Nobel Prize winners Crick and Watson in the 1960s when they co-discovered the double-helical structure of DNA – the chemical that carries hereditary characteristics from generation to generation. In this particular reading the spirit decided he could only prove that he was well and functioning to his daughter by specifically referring to the building blocks of life itself! In my professional opinion (and other mediums may differ) the reason that spirits do not explain secrets of a divine nature is that it is not their main priority. Their needs are simple: they wish to contact their loved ones with two primary messages. Firstly, to tell them that that they are OK, and secondly, that those who are still grieving should accept their death and carry on with their lives.

The spirits also perform a valuable function in that they often help me detect the emotional state of those for whom I read. This can often be divided up into several key emotional areas:

- **Anger**. Often there is anger at things said or left unsaid. Many feel that there were things they wish they could have said to their loved ones, or wish they had heard from them. Sometimes there is anger at physical circumstances, e.g. a traffic jam that might have prevented a final visit, or the unjustness of an accidental death. Anger is often directed at a different source to its cause.

- **Guilt**. People are often guilt-ridden over things left unfinished or unsaid. Sometimes people feel guilty for being happy that somebody they loved died quickly rather than lingering in pain. Sometimes there is guilt as people think that they 'could have done more' when the person was still alive.

- **Depression**. When you lose a loved one there is an obvious void which cannot be filled and which confronts you from the moment you wake up until you sleep. Even when you accept bereavement and move on, feelings of emptiness and loneliness will remain for a considerable period of time.

- **Numbness**. A person who is grieving will feel dazed and numb – the feeling can be compared to trying to walk the wrong way through a wind tunnel. When someone we have always taken for granted is suddenly no longer there, a certain lack of sensation can occupy the brain.

- **Confusion.** Confusion can be both practical and mental. You have to make funeral arrangements, put things in order and do a certain amount of physical tidying up after a person passes over. This can be difficult and extremely time-consuming. Plus there is the mental anguish and floods of memory that usually accompany these activities.

- **Fear.** People are naturally afraid or apprehensive about facing the future without a loved one with whom they've shared a significant past. There is also a personal fear that kicks in as you are reminded about your own mortality.

Mostly, though, the spirits detect in their loved ones a combination of these emotions. All of these feelings are manifestations of unfinished emotional business. I have found that very few people are actually in denial. People whom I get to see are fully aware that their loved one has passed on. They are very clear that there has been a death, but what they are trying to do is come to terms with it. I always say to people that thank goodness we cannot regulate when we die and that we do not live in some science fiction nightmare where the state can decide. Human beings have free will and are bound only to the laws of nature. The results of this freedom, though, are the swirling mass of complex feelings and emotion that accompany bereavement. That is why the majority of the messages I receive are simply spirits trying to help turn their loved one's confused and sometimes negative emotions into more positive ones.

## In death we are all equal

One of the most important things I want to say in this book is that I have never detected a hierarchy amongst the spirits who contact me. By this I mean there seem to be no judgements as to how people died, at what age they died and what they did with their lives on earth. Spirits are not placed in a pecking order – they just come through as needed. The reason I say this is to emphasise that spirits who took their own lives and come through are not in some kind of no man's land. In fact, in almost all cases I'm glad to say their wounded state of mind has healed. That is my experience. In instances where someone has taken their own life a spirit will sometimes tell me immediately while others will force me to draw the information out.

I started one particular reading with the immediate knowledge that I was dealing with a young man who had taken his own life. He was very forthright and directed me to the row in which his mother and sisters were sitting.

'I need to come to you and tell you immediately that your son and brother is OK,' I said. I couldn't focus on a name so I tried to confirm that I was with the right people in another way.

'Would one of his sisters remember a photograph of you and your brother where one of you is wearing a kilt or a tartan skirt?'

One of the sisters smiled and said, 'I've got a picture. It's of all of us together, he's a baby and I've got a red tartan skirt on.'

This spirit had no difficulty in speaking to me. He knew what he had to say and who he needed to say it to. As in all these cases I explained to this family sitting in the audience that I knew about the circumstances of death and would stop giving the message if they wanted. They asked me to carry on.

'For two years before I did it I felt tainted. I will never understand how someone can do that to somebody but I have come to terms with it.'

He showed me an old man with him and I acknowledged that when he passed over, he was met by his grandfather who took care of him. 'He hopes that you all take a lot of comfort in the knowledge that he and granddad spend a lot of time at the pond just fishing.

'He's not sure if you knew this but he had tried twice before, and he is telling me that it is very important that he explains to you that on the third occasion when he did finally take his earthly life, he had planned it out.'

He started showing me a book. Was it something he liked reading? No. I concentrated harder. 'He appreciates the words that you all put in the book; Mum, would you understand that you have made a collection of things to remember him at his best?'

His mother nodded. 'I wrote his story.'

He asked me to tell his sisters something: 'He's telling me something amusing for you both. Until such time that you are all over there at least he won't have to endure the embarrassment of you two trying to get him to dance!'

I could sense my communicator moving away.

'The last thing is for you, Mum. In the book you wrote words to the effect of *I know my boy is happier there than he could have been here.* He wants to tell you that this is true. Especially now, now he is safe and well and is no longer a victim.'

I left his love with his family.

The mother told the story to one of the producers. She actually said that she knew I was going to come over to her a few seconds before I did. She just felt a surge of electricity go though her body and knew. She explained that her son James had taken his life several years earlier. He had been assaulted in a car park and, after regaining consciousness, had tried to drive home. Seeing an erratic driver the police stopped him and then arrested and charged him with dangerous driving. James went into a deep depression from which he never recovered, feeling that he was being treated as a criminal and not the victim of an assault. Two years later he took his own life after two failed attempts.

After his death his mother wrote a book telling the story of his life, collated from family contributions. She explained that it was highly significant to her why he had come through at this point in time, as two weeks previously a BBC radio programme convinced the police to admit that they had made mistakes when dealing with the case and had apologised on air to James's family and friends. As a child he had loved fishing with his grandfather and the woman was happy to know that that was where James was now.

Like all interviewees on the show she was asked by the producer what the reading had meant to her. She replied that he might be content but that justice had prevailed a little too late for the rest of the family. Her overriding concern was that he was finally at peace, and she felt that now she would be able to add one last chapter to James's memorial book.

## Suicide does not exclude a spiritual connection

This may be controversial but as a spiritualist medium I disagree strongly with the beliefs of many people who claim that the souls of those who commit suicide are punished on the other side. I do not wish to change anybody's existing religious beliefs, but I'm not afraid to state what I believe. Mediums seem to have no difficulty receiving messages from those who took their own life (nor, might I add, from those who lost their faith or babies who were not baptised etc.). I do understand that people inherit or adopt accepted beliefs, but my experience has always been that these spirits are not lost at all; instead they are helped by the world of spirit to be at peace with those issues that they could never have been at peace with on this side of life.

Some of my most heart-wrenching and meaningful readings have been with the families and friends of those who have committed suicide. They feel that few others can relate to their grief and the subject is so very difficult for them to talk about. They permanently feel that their loved one eliminated the chance for a solution. Acting as a go-between, a medium can allow them to express their anger and conflicting feelings towards their lost loved one as emotions run high. Don't get me wrong, my bottom line here is not that suicide was the right thing for a person to do; just that it was the result of an imbalance of pain versus coping resources.

Let me state that again – I do NOT condone suicide. However, it is also not right that we live in societies where people feel both emotionally and physically that there is no place for them in this world. This not only reflects on the person, but also on those societies themselves. Ultimately there are a lot of people that pass over into the spirit world after taking their own life and I am utterly convinced they are the recipients of more compassion for them on that side of life than there was for them on this side.

## Finding inspiration in death

I'd like to end this chapter by stressing that the manner in which a person dies is far less important than the inspirational force they can leave with their loved ones. If a person who passes motivates you to do good things with your life, then it can be said that they haven't died at all but are kept alive by your actions. In my life this is certainly true. I have explained how I started out giving readings for friends as a party piece, and then was adopted by a development circle, generated controversy through physical mediumship and eventually was lucky to perform in front of larger audiences both in theatres and on TV. But what was the key event that made me give up the security of being in retail management and become a full-time professional medium? It was a person. His name was Michael.

I knew Michael from my teens and considered myself lucky to have been his friend for over twenty years. Michael had gone to the same school as my mother, although he was several years younger. He was a Barnado's boy who had been through a great deal and my family helped look after him during his adolescence. I met him in my teens and he proved to be both a good friend to my parents and a mentor for me. He was an intimidating character, of enormous physical build, and with a mysterious security job that he couldn't talk about, but one that required him to sign the Official Secrets Act! He was my protector, and in my early twenties prevented me from getting into any worse trouble than I did. He taught me about the pitfalls of the gay scene and how ruthless it could be. Michael also helped me come out to my parents, which they handled well. He was an older brother and mentor rolled into one. I particularly loved his sense of humour. Michael acknowledged he was not the best-looking person around by saying it was his great misfortune to be 'young and beautiful'.

When he reached his early fifties, Michael seemed to suddenly get very fatigued. He gave up his top-secret job and took a little job driving for a local bakery. By this time I was getting increasingly concerned about how exhausted and unwell he seemed. One day I received an urgent phone call. He had been rushed into hospital. In fact he'd not been rushed to the nearest general hospital but to Hove General, which I knew had a special ward for people with HIV and Aids. Remember this was in the early history of the disease when not a great deal was known about it – and certain drugs had not been tested so people with HIV struggled as best they could. While he was in the hospital Michael said to me, 'I am going to get very ill. I have no family so would you take my power of attorney?' Naturally I accepted.

Michael went home, but not surprisingly he became depressed. One day I received a phone call telling me he'd been rushed to hospital again. This turned out to be a local psychiatric hospital. When I arrived I could see poor Michael sitting there in what can only be described as a room of seriously disturbed people. This was not where he was going to die. The psychiatrist would not let me take him home but I finally told her that she shouldn't mess with me and I was getting him out of there. I took him home, where he managed to live for eight years. His attitude and unselfishness were extraordinary.

Michael knew he was virtually a guinea pig for some of the early HIV drug treatments but he still took them even though he knew that it was too late to save him. He told me, 'If they save someone else then my death will not be in vain.'

I was privileged to help look after him as he became seriously ill. We used to joke about us being brothers. A couple of weeks before he passed he had bypass surgery, but could no longer sustain his blood pressure. I was called to the hospital where Michael was lying in bed, connected to machines and with tubes coming out of him. He passed over as I and another friend held his hands.

There is no doubt that the end of this friendship changed my perspective on life. I felt unable to return to my job and found life quite meaningless. However, after several days of being in the dumps I realised that my behaviour was ultimately very selfish. Knowing how his death had affected me I started to focus on how his passing must have affected others. I knew that his spirit had not died, and that he had passed over, but what of others who were unable to have this proved to them? This became my motivation to pursue a life of mediumship. It was my job to provide evidence of the continuation of spirit to those who were seeking it.

I announced to my partner that I wasn't going to go back to work. My colleagues thought I needed a break, but my mind was very clear on the matter. I realised that my mediumship needed to be more important than a hobby and that I had to make full use of this gift. One of the key ways that I made sense of Michael's passing was to use my mediumship as a full-time occupation rather than a part-time hobby. The funny thing was that two days after he passed I saw him in my mirror when I was shaving, laughing at me. I asked him if I was making the right decision and he simply smiled and told me to concentrate on the razor!

I consider my work to be a tribute to him and all the other friends and family I've lost over the years. I know what's happened to them and I've sometimes had communication from them. On other occasions I've had messages via other mediums. I know life carries on as I've had evidence of it almost every day of my life and I just want to pass some of that on to other people. I suppose that my commitment to being a full-time medium was really my way of paying tribute to Michael and everyone else who was a part of my life before they passed.

## Accepting and coping with death

- By not talking about death we may lose our chance to make the most of the time we have with someone who is dying. It will be difficult but it will mean that when they do die we will know we did our best.
- It is important to grieve for the loss. We are putting off that process if we keep asking, 'Why?' Instead we need to accept that death has happened and attempt to incorporate the event into our lives.
- There is no template for grief. It is intensely personal and only you can work out your method of coping with the loss of a loved one. It may take time: grief has a beginning but there is no middle and end.
- When the physical body dies, a person's spirit continues as an integral part of the spirit world that exists, but in a different dimension to our world.
- We are all equal in death. Even if a person has committed suicide there is no reason why their spirit should not be at rest. Similarly there is no reason why their loved ones cannot feel good about them even if they do not feel good about the manner of their death.
- Death can be an inspiration to continue with life. We shall explore this in the next chapter.

# 8.

# Living: life after a death

*'Live life as a tribute to those who have borne you, raised you, befriended you and cherished you.'*

**MAGNUS, SPIRIT GUIDE TO COLIN FRY**

In the previous chapter I discussed the need to treat death as a part of life. I spoke about the importance of being able to talk about it openly so that we are better able to come to terms with it ourselves and to help others do so. Here I want to go one step further and discuss how we can use death in order to affirm life so that we move forward in a more fulfilling way. Although you will feel sadness and loss, they do not have to be the only things that bereavement leaves you with. No matter how painful and deep the loss we have suffered, I believe we can continue to grow by using our memories of loved ones to motivate us and make us stronger. In fact I'll go one step further and say it's your responsibility to do so. The greatest insult we can give to those who have passed is when we decide not to carry on with our own lives. It doesn't matter whether you believe in the afterlife or not: life after death is open to all of us. Having said that, there is much to learn from the spirit world about how we can conduct ourselves.

## Is there anything out there?

Let's first deal with one question that I know many readers will want to ask at this point. 'Colin, how can you be so sure that there really is a spirit world?' To me the answer is simple – I can sense it, or more importantly, I can sense the spirits around me who contact me with the aim of passing on messages to their loved ones. This book cannot prove this to you or open a magic window to the spirit world, but I have seen these spirits ever since I was a small child. I wish I could describe to you what it looks like but the truth is I and other mediums can only understand it in human terms. We tend to give it characteristics that we know from our own experiences and if I'm honest then I'm not sure how accurate a description could really be. All I can say is that it is not some toy town with bright colours or a place where angels play harps sitting on fluffy clouds. However, the great healer and medium Harry Edwards once said that 'all mediumship is a mirror of the mind' so it may well be that some people perceive the spirit world in that way.

There have been many articles published by people who have had near-death experiences and claim to have glimpsed views of the afterlife. These tend to be cases of people who are pronounced 'medically dead' in a hospital, but then recover consciousness. They often claim to have floated upwards and seen their bodies as well as other people in the room from above. They can often recall conversations that went on around them. Some have even related details of events taking place in different locations at the same time. Most of these people also tell of being drawn towards a very bright light and heading down a tunnel towards angel-like beings; many too recall being told things such as, 'It is not your time yet', before regaining consciousness.

To me none of this seems particularly mysterious. It reflects my true belief that only a person's physical body dies, i.e. stops functioning, but their spirit moves on to a higher spirit world. Dying does not mean we cease to exist when our body ceases to function, it means that our consciousness or spirit, which does not depend on physical support, is able to move on to the spirit world. I think sometimes that we are similar to caterpillars. After we die we shed our skin (i.e. bodies) and grow into something more or something bigger. There is a Spirit World out there, where our souls can grow and continue to develop from the point at which they left their earthly life.

## Use death to affirm life

I can honestly say that when I speak to souls in the spirit world I never feel a sense of sadness in their communications with me. They do not convey a sense of melancholy that they are leaving their loved ones here on earth. In fact quite often there is almost a bit of amusement about this perception by the living from their places in the spirit world because for them life has gone on. In the same way that several years after a person has died the relatives will have moved on, so too is it for those in the spirit world. There is nothing for them to mourn over. The only sadness they feel is for their loved ones who have not come to terms with their passing or are still grieving inconsolably for them. I believe they do miss us, but in a completely different way to how we miss them. I feel that they are obviously able to connect to our lives much more ably than we can connect to theirs, but they do not feel the same sense of loss that we do. It is thus essential to somehow keep our loved ones 'alive' in our lives so that we don't feel that perpetual sense of separation or loss.

I knew it was the spirit of a young child because he told me he didn't have a name. 'Tell Mum that I passed at five past two.'

I have to be honest and say that I tried to suppress a tear. A little baby coming forward to say hello to its mum or dad will almost always reduce me to tears no matter how many similar readings I have given in the past.

I told Kelly and Dean what was being shown to me. We were in a room at the theatre in Rhyl and I was giving a 'one-to-one' a few hours before that evening's demonstration. Before me sat a very brave couple who were yearning for a special message.

'This little child is showing me blue balloons,' I said.

'That's what we had filled the room with,' said Dean, his eyes shining brightly.

For some reason I began to see another, bigger boy of about eight years old playing football. 'I think he has an older brother,' I said.

The couple nodded at me.

'He's a bit naughty, this one! I think he tried to feed a sandwich into a video player once!'

Kelly began to smile.

'Honestly,' I said, 'he's showing me this little boy put bread into a video recorder – I think he broke it!'

I continued, 'He knows this little boy is too young to understand, but he looks over him when he plays football.'

I tried to get more information from this little spirit. 'There is an older woman with him. She's holding his hand. This older woman is showing me that she was there when he passed over. What's the significance of 17 March?' I asked.

Kelly managed to say, 'It was my mother's birthday,' before she burst into floods of tears. All of us were very emotional.

'This lady is in spirit, isn't she?' I looked at Kelly, but I already sensed I was correct. 'She is looking after your little boy.'

I tried to get more information. When one passes so young, there are virtually no memories or recollections.

'He's telling me he's glad you took photographs in the end. That's how he wants you to think of him, not what the doctors did afterwards.'

Even though we were all crying at this point, I tried to stay centred and get as much information as possible. I had a job to do, even if I was feeling sad.

'Before he goes he says he thinks the idea of you losing weight is funny.' I didn't mean to be offensive, but that was the message. 'Especially as you help other people put weight on!'

'He says that Dad is also trying to help, but it doesn't involve losing weight.' I felt this communication drawing to a close. There was one last message he had wanted to pass on. 'Your little boy says that he knows you were with him.'

As I kept passing around the tissues and trying to control my own tears, Kelly and Dean told me their heart-rending story, that even before their son was born they knew he was suffering from a rare genetic disorder. The doctors decided that owing to further complications it would endanger Kelly's life to terminate the pregnancy, so she had gone through labour and given birth in the knowledge that her son only had a few hours to live.

The doctors tried to make things as painless as possible, but indeed several hours after the birth the child had passed away in their arms.

'He was beautiful,' said Kelly, desperately trying to smile through her tears. A mother's pain is very difficult to watch.

I felt so helpless, as I often do in these situations. All I could offer was this message, but it proved to be accurate enough for them to believe it had been their child coming through and speaking to me. He did indeed have a football-mad older brother who had tried to feed the big mouth on the video with jam sandwiches. They had specifically filled the room with blue balloons and they had taken several photos, knowing that the hospital was required to perform an autopsy on the baby's body.

Dean explained, 'We set up a trust in his memory so that we could raise money for further research into genetic defects.' Kelly worked as a lunch lady in a local care home and was planning on going on a sponsored diet to raise more funds.

I was exceptionally glad to be able to bring them such a message and although it left me somewhat emotionally drained, it actually put me in a good frame of mind before the big show that evening. I didn't bring up this story to show you that I can cry, but because the behaviour of Dean and Kelly is such a good example of those looking to give meaning to their lives after a tragedy.

I have given many readings to those who have lost children, whether through illness, accident, or miscarriage, and I've seen so many parents find solace in dedicating help to others in the name of their loved ones. Keeping alive their memory in such a way is something for which I have nothing but the greatest admiration. Of course these people would never have chosen their circumstances, but by giving others their love and compassion they are discovering a new layer of meaning to life.

As I said in the introduction to this book, people think mediums are obsessed with death. Actually we are not. The dead are fine, honest I know – I speak with them every day. It's the living we are obsessed with, trying to help them. One reading very much stands out in my mind. A woman came once with her brother for a sitting with me. She accepted that I wanted to receive no background information, but handed me a ring and asked me to hold it during the reading to see if it helped me pick up on any particular vibrations. I agreed. She gave me a man's sovereign ring, which I felt gingerly between my fingers and started to concentrate on and *psychometrise*. It is not a pretty word but its meaning is simple.

A major tool available to psychics and mediums is that of *psychometry*. This is the ability to define the character, surroundings and influences of an article. The psychic picks up an object such as a piece of jewellery or an item of clothing and, by handling the object, will try to discern facts such as information about the owner and describe the relationship between him or her and the object. The impressions received can vary in intensity. Like the use of crystals, psychometry is a useful tool for focusing the mind and making connections with the spirit world.

I linked my mind into this ring and at once had a very clear impression. I said, 'The boy who owned this ring worked in the brickworks.'

The lady nodded in agreement.

More information came through. I picked up on the boy's name and on the fact that this boy was supposed to have committed suicide, but somehow it didn't feel at all right. Situations like this are very tricky and you have to be thoughtful about what you say.

The lady was very pleased with the sitting, especially as I had picked up on the boy's name, the fact that he was her son, and various other key pieces of family information.

'Can I return to see you with my husband?' she asked at the end of the reading. 'I think he needs to come.'

I said, 'Yes, of course.' Despite seeming 'together' she was obviously still grieving terribly for the passing of her son, and I knew that there was something mysterious about his death. A few weeks later she returned, this time accompanied by her husband, who barely spoke a word. This time I concentrated on finding out exactly how the boy had passed.

Once again I used the ring to make a link with this spirit and he chose to answer our call.

'I feel like this boy is a little embarrassed about saying what he has to say.'

The lady did not seem perturbed or surprised. 'Can you find out why, please?' I sensed this woman just wanted some truth.

Each time I reached out with my mind to feel for more information the spirit changed the subject. He was very evasive indeed. When he eventually told me what had happened I was not sure whether to pass these facts on to his parents.

'I know that people thought I tried to commit suicide but it's not true. The real story is that I accidentally hanged myself – I used to get a kick out of trying it.'

'Oh dear,' I thought. 'This is definitely not the sort of thing grieving parents want to hear. What shall I do?' I tried to skirt around the issue, feeling acutely uncomfortable talking about these things in front of the boy's parents, but when the mother said pleadingly, 'Just tell us, Colin. I know you know,' I had no choice.

I remember that when I finally came out and told them what their son was showing me she just let out a huge sigh of relief and said, 'We knew that was what had happened; we couldn't accept that he committed suicide but we just needed to hear it from him.'

It taught me a valuable lesson as to what mediumship was all about. My job was to pass on the message, not to worry about its meaning. I had almost not transferred the very information his parents needed in order to give them a chance to go away and start repairing their lives. Now that they had heard it, they could certainly move onwards in the grieving process. They may still have had a lot to go through but the important thing was that they were making an effort to move on. And that is what we all need to do.

I cannot remember all the readings I've ever given, word for word. I don't think that mediums are meant to retain all of these things, as they do not represent anything personal to us. We are just the givers of the message. However, there are always those messages over the years that remain in my mind either due to their emotional content or the impact that the message has had on its recipients. One such reading stands out.

It was a private sitting with a lady called Claire. I began by sensing a gentle elderly man trying to connect with me. I received the information that in the latter part of his earthly life he had had a problem with his eyes being very watery.

'He also tells me that he was only supposed to eat certain things. I can hear someone telling him off for hiding a bag of sweets in his pocket!'

Claire said, 'Probably my mum – she was always finding them.'

I continued. 'Would you understand about somebody that accidentally flushed some money down a toilet or put money in a water cistern?'

Claire laughed. She had quite a hearty laugh. 'Not a toilet, but I think I know what he's talking about.'

I couldn't see exactly what it was, but I told her that I saw an extremely large amount of money – at least £1,000 – being washed away in a lot of swirling water.

'I can smell a sort of burning,' I continued. 'I have a distinct vision of you ironing out all this money; talk about money laundering!'

Claire said 'Grandpa thought it was hilarious!'

He showed me an image of Disney's *Snow White and the Seven Dwarfs*. 'Was it a film he took you to when he was younger?' I distinctly saw him watching this film with a little girl.

'It wasn't me,' she replied. 'When he used to be over at my house sometimes, with my children, one of their favourite films was *Snow White* – they used to watch it over and over again.'

Up to this point the reading had been a nice gentle affair with some pleasant anecdotes, but at this point I remember the mood changing and things feeling more sombre. I realised that Claire's granddad was intending to act as an 'enabler' for a younger spirit who also desired to come through that day.

'I feel that my friend here is helping another soul come

through and make the connection today. This other spirit is a very sensitive, artistic person, a person you instinctively knew you wanted to handle more gently than other people because you knew that the slightest thing might hurt them.'

As I was talking I could see the most beautiful eyes, and I realised that Claire would have done anything to protect this child.

'I've got to be honest with you – the feeling that she's giving me is that she's a daughter or a younger sister. I say that because I feel that people might have seen the two of you together and they wouldn't have known you were mother and daughter. You behaved as if you were best friends, or even two very close sisters.'

The laughter was gone now. Claire wiped the tears from her eyes. 'She's my daughter, Colin. But she was always there for me like a sister. She was my best friend, and no-one or anything will ever replace her, it can't.'

Now that the daughter had made contact through me with the help of her grandfather, she started passing on her own messages. She put an image in my mind of a beautiful girl in a classic ballet pose.

'Have you got a photograph of her in a very elegant ballet pose? Because she's just said that's our picture.'

It would not have been an exaggeration to say that Claire went a deathly white, as she nodded in confirmation.

This spirit showed me a boy that she had been close with. 'She's showing me a sensitive boy, I don't know if it's a boyfriend, but he has cried too many tears. You must tell him to get back on the rails and be himself.'

Claire said that she would.

I realised that the communication was drawing to a close,

but I sensed that there was something Claire was waiting for. Some piece of information that might affect the way she looked at her life. I concentrated very hard, knowing instinctively that the outcome would be important.

I looked at the lady opposite me and gave her the words being put into my head. 'They're just bits, Mum. Just bits.' I felt that she had had a chance conversation with Claire a few weeks before she passed, something to do with donor cards, and she had said the same thing to her at the time.

'Mum, they're only bits.'

Claire looked up at me and said, 'Good. That's all I wanted to know.'

I know it sounds like a bit of a cliché, but the atmosphere changed in that room. As the daughter's spirit started to depart she referred to the gentleman who first came in at the beginning of the reading and said, 'Don't worry, Mum, we actually look after one another.' She left her love with her mother, and with that my mind went blank.

Over strong coffee (we needed it!) Claire helped me to understand the significance of her reading. The gentleman with the watery eyes was Claire's grandfather. He had diabetes and he used to love sherbet lemons, often begging her to go and buy him some. 'I'd get him a bag and nine times out of ten my mum would find them in his pocket and give him such earache, but he never told on me ever. Now when my mum hears about this I'm in real trouble!'

One day Claire had accidentally washed a pair of her husband's jeans with £1,200 in cash in one of the pockets. She found out because he happened to call in the middle of the wash and asked about his trousers. Claire remembers trying to remove all the notes without damaging them and putting them on the radiator with her grandfather watching. They even tried to iron the money afterwards. Her grandfather would often watch *Snow White* with her children when they were small but in particular with her daughter.

Claire said, 'At this point I was just hoping that this was a reference to my daughter and that she was starting to come through.'

Her fourteen-year-old daughter had died just over a year prior to the reading. She had been a healthy, happy-go-lucky child, who was out one day and tragically collapsed with a brain haemorrhage. She passed away several hours later.

Claire told me that ever since her pregnancy she had possessed a fear of losing a child and continually tried to protect her daughter against everything. The part of the reading that had almost caused her to faint was about the picture of a ballet dancer. Six weeks before her daughter collapsed, Claire had promised her a locket of hers, but had never got round to giving it to her. Before the funeral Claire put a picture of a ballet dancer in the locket, took it down to the chapel and put it around her daughter's neck. She was buried with this locket!

She also had a boyfriend who was with her when she collapsed, and was with Claire in the hospital afterwards. Claire promised to tell him what her daughter had asked and hoped that it would help him to overcome his grief.

She explained to me that after her daughter had passed she had donated her organs, saving five children, but had suffered in torment ever since, agonising over whether she had made the right decision.

'I just needed to hear it from her,' she said. To which all I could reply was, 'You did. You did.'

The story has lovely postscript. A few weeks later Claire

attended one of the television show tapings. I asked her how she was getting on and she said that it was as if a weight had been lifted from her shoulders. The impact it had had on her family was also considerable, and it was helping all of them to come to terms with what had happened. It left me feeling particularly warm. I too have no comprehension of how and why such tragedies happen, but at least I was able to offer proof that her daughter's spirit continued to live long after it had outgrown a use for its body. Now Claire and her family were able to move on from wondering what their daughter would have thought and instead concentrate on dealing with helping and supporting each other as they tried to recover from their heartbreak.

What Claire and her family had done was to use their daughter's tragic death to try and put their own lives in perspective. In doing so they were also celebrating the life of their daughter. It is very important for us to remember and celebrate the life of a loved one. Of course this is liable to stir up strong feelings and memories, but it will enable us to relive our past and help place it into a proper perspective. This exercise might also challenge you to ask, 'How could my relationship have been different?' and this can be emotionally draining. However, this is the pain we are forced to address if we are to make progress in resolving our grief. Simply articulating our regrets and our disappointed hopes can be a great release. Not only that but it helps us to truly value our ability to remember. The strong feelings of grief and sadness are ultimately the most positive statement you can make about the deceased as it says these people had a unique value. They were precious to your world and contributed to who you are today and this will determine how you honour their memory and legacy.

In a strange way the realisation of these things – admissions of loss and what exactly your loss means to you – will act as a way of providing a stronger sense of what it means to be alive and living in the present. Once you have confronted your feelings, the burdens of the past take up less space in your mind, and you will feel less weighed down.

## Use your powers of positive thinking

Remember what we talked about in chapter 2: we are what we think. If we say things such as, '*What is the purpose of living when our loved ones are not here?*', then our words and our thoughts will dictate our life. If we say things such as, '*I'll never get over it*', then we probably never will. We have to think our way positively through our grief. Feelings of '*I can't change*' will mean just that, and the one thing that you are guaranteed to have to deal with after the loss of a loved one is change.

I think there is an important principle to accept if you do indeed believe in a form of afterlife or the continuation of a person's spirit. If you are of the opinion that there is an afterlife, then it is simply disrespectful to our loved ones if we do not move forward at some point with our own lives. You need to shift the question from, 'How do I stop feeling overcome with grief?' to 'How do I continue with my life in such a way that it shows respect for that person who has passed on?'

Many years ago I gave a reading that helped illustrate this point for me. I met up with a couple called Andrew and Barbara. They had told me that they wished to contact a child who had passed to the spirit world, but beyond that I had no other background information.

As I began the 'one-to-one' I began to feel moving and shuddering sensations. I felt like I was passing through a tunnel.

It was as if I was in a car that suddenly went into a tunnel and as I came out of the dark I saw before me a row of different soft toys. In the middle was a stuffed Paddington Bear. I tried to focus on what this child looked like but instead saw a young adult. For some reason he was showing me this Paddington Bear.

I explained what I was feeling, in particular seeing a row of stuffed toys, but it provoked no real response in my clients. I focused harder.

'I get the sense of one who passed very quickly – almost in a flash. One minute he was in this world – the next he wasn't.' I saw the young man walking down a road with a rucksack on his back and had the sensation of one who was off to school.

'This boy really liked school.'

'Yes, very much,' said Andrew.

Something wasn't quite right here and I became very conscious of letting my spirit down. I needed confirmation that this man did indeed want to come through and speak to this couple.

'Yes,' he said. He showed me images of him working at a desk. He had lots of textbooks open in front of him and was writing into a notebook by the light of a table lamp.

I realised the mistake I was making. This young man was their child, but by concentrating on the child's toy I had assumed he had passed over as a child, but this wasn't the case. He had passed over as a young adult. So what was the significance of Paddington? A spirit will try and identify itself to its loved ones by conveying information to me that is important – so what did it all actually mean?

I was back in the tunnel again, only this time when I emerged out of the other side I heard a large 'bang'.

'I know this sounds strange,' I said, 'but I think your boy was in some sort of train crash. He was on the way to school and was hit by a train.'

Relief showed clearly on their faces. Relief then tears.

He gave me several childhood memories, which his parents confirmed as being true, and showed me the Paddington Bear toy once more. 'I mentioned some stuffed toys before, but I need to stress one particular toy he keeps on showing me – that of Paddington Bear.'

'He died in the Paddington rail disaster,' said Barbara, her eyes welling up with tears.

Now I understood fully. He showed me that he had been a student and had died on the way to college. I asked for more detailed clarification. He told me that he had been studying chemistry and had hoped to become an engineer. Unlike many spirits who give me memories, this one was more comfortable giving me detailed descriptions of his aims and plans for the future had he not passed so tragically.

'But that was him exactly,' said his mother.

'He's very glad that Dad came.'

Andrew nodded.

'There is a special message he'd like to tell you.' Andrew stared hard at me. I'm not sure whether he was trying not to cry.

'It was me who died, Dad, not you.'

I watched his troubled face. This last part of the message was startlingly to the point, almost offensive. I had to make sure that he was willing for me to continue, even if it meant saying something that I felt might be too shocking.

'He always said what was on his mind, so I don't see why now should be any different,' said Andrew.

So I concluded his message: 'He says that you will die one day, Dad! Don't worry, I promise you, you will, but in the meantime don't forget that I died in the crash, not you!'

I have to admit I was half expecting Andrew to hit me, or at least have one of them get up and walk out, but instead Barbara looked to Andrew and said, 'He's right, you know he's always right!' I felt a huge sense of relief from them.

After the message ended we all felt the need to talk it over. Unlike many people who come to see me, Andrew and Barbara had always believed in the continuation of their son's spirit and the fact that I'd spoken to him made little impression in itself, but the final point he'd made to his father had.

'It all happened a few years ago, but it's true that I felt that I too died that day. He had been such a promising student, with his whole life ahead of him and then in an instant all of that was gone.'

I asked him if he felt he could pinpoint the specific cause of these feelings.

'It was me who put him on the train. I always felt it was my fault. I should have suggested he take a later train. What if I had driven him to college instead ...?' His voice trailed off.

I explained that in my opinion this was what the son was referring to in his message. It was this guilt at being unable to protect his son against the unforeseen and the unstoppable that was paralysing Andrew's will to live. So many times have I read for people who torture themselves over what they might have done to save somebody. The reality is that they couldn't and are achieving nothing by beating themselves up about it.

I said to Andrew, 'You believe that your son's spirit has continued and you believe that he came through to me today; he's shown you how he wants to see you, not dead to the world, but living your own life to the full.'

Andrew nodded slowly then put his head in his hands. It might have looked like despair, but I felt that this might be a new beginning for him.

The message that comforted this couple is a good one for all of us. It matters not only what you think as a grieving person, but you also have to ask yourself, 'What would my loved one think?' and 'How would they expect me to think?' It is only natural that a grieving person feels they are stuck in some sort of rut. That's what loss does to you. My work has shown me that our loved ones do not require us to grieve indefinitely over their passing. Ask yourself, how would you want your loved one to see you now? I can tell you that not only would they not want you to be dead to the world, they would rather see you honour their lives by carrying on with your life. If you don't, then it's you who have died, not them.

A person with no belief in the continuation of spirit would simply say that you must accept that a person has died, put them to one side and now get on with your life. As a medium I feel a different truth. Yes you must acknowledge the fact that a person has put aside their physical existence, but you must also acknowledge that that person still exists as a life force.

If you have love and respect for them then you will still keep them as part of your life.

When I first embarked on my life as a psychic medium I remember being filled with a strange combination of extreme self-confidence and also extreme self-doubt. On the one hand I was absolutely sure that this was my calling – that I had been put on this earth in order to use my gift to pass on as many messages as I would be allowed, and yet at the same time I was filled with dread – what if the messages stopped coming or weren't accurate? As I've already mentioned, I studied to become a bereavement counsellor. I reasoned with myself that at least this way if the spirits stopped coming through I would have something to fall back on. Luckily this has not been the case – I have been blessed with these abilities and someone seems to be looking after me from above. There is however one very big difference between giving a reading and giving bereavement counselling. During the former I do not want the person sitting opposite me to tell me a thing and during the latter I ask them to tell me anything they want. When trying to pass on a message I want to minimise the risk of a misunderstanding, so the less I know about the person and who they are hoping to hear from the better. This way when a loved one does come through the impact is much greater and I cannot be accused of simply pandering to the person's needs. During counselling, however, I want to hear as much about the person's loss as they are prepared to tell me. The ability to communicate our emotions openly and clearly, happy or sad, is one of the distinguishing characteristics of being human.

## Coping with feelings of guilt

One of the saddest readings I ever gave involved a teenage boy who, just before joining the army cadets, was impaled on a metal spike while playing with some friends in what can only be described as a million-to-one freak accident. The nature of the boy's passing left his parents with no-one to blame or take the responsibility. Unfortunately they found themselves blaming each other for something that they could have had no control over. It is basic human nature to blame someone or something for the bad things that happen to us in life rather than 'manage' them. In some cases we can apportion the blame squarely and directly, and in others we can blame our circumstances or bad timing. Here we cannot. As we spoke about in the previous chapter, when bad things do happen to us, we must try to let go of the resentment and anger we feel, and not keep them within us for ever. This poor couple's perceived guilt was damaging their lives beyond repair.

Perhaps a lack of guilt in our lives (like periods of suffering) is also an unreal expectation. It too must be managed correctly. Guilt is a powerful and destructive weapon when used against us. It restricts us until it shuts us down. The truth is that no-one can beat us up better than ourselves for things that we have actually done and things that we haven't. However, you simply cannot progress in life if you are whipping yourself in shame. Perhaps I can offer a few personal rules that may help in managing life a bit better. They work on the assumption that we have to set ourselves aims and goals in life, that all of us will have setbacks, and that no-one can have a perfect life:

## Five steps to managing guilt (one step at a time)

- Know full well what you have done in the past.
- Understand the implications of that action.
- Try to make restitution.
- Ask for forgiveness if you have hurt another.
- Resolve to change your future behaviour.

Taking responsibility for our mistakes is redeeming and positive, but feeling guilty has absolutely no value. It does not encourage us to change in positive ways but debilitates us, leaving us unable to take the action we need to bring about change. It often becomes a self-perpetuating cycle: we do something wrong which we feel guilt about, we punish ourselves and then because we feel emotionally unstable, we end up repeating our behaviour at the next available chance.

In cases where we have hurt someone, making amends is more than just saying sorry. It involves a willingness to listen to another person's hurt and take corrective action where possible. We and our relationships must be transformed as we change our future behaviour patterns. I am not implying that a bad action can be pushed under the carpet. I believe in the laws of spiritual cause and effect. We still have to live with the consequences of anything we do; at the same time no-one is beyond redeeming their past actions, and making amends in the correct manner will add more meaning and purpose to the remainder of our lives.

So many people come to see me for 'one-to-ones' and say that they have to speak with somebody because they never got round to saying what they wanted to say, or that they now feel they could have done more to alleviate their suffering. I see people literally haunted by guilt – sometimes real, but all too often imagined. In most cases I say, 'What more should you have done?' Most of the conditions could not have been changed. Most people simply tried to cope the best they could under the circumstances. Even in cases where people did wrong to a person who has passed, I can say that the person has forgiven them. There is no need for them to continue to hate and bear resentment in the spirit world; however, let me go out on a limb here and say that part of managing your life is understanding that our physical bodies do not last indefinitely. Resolve any arguments or disagreements that you have with family members right here and right now. I would rather you put me out of a job, than punish yourself with guilt later!

As I said before, even I cannot contact any spirit I want, whenever I want. So let me share the secret of how I stay in touch with those I have loved and lost. It has nothing to do with being a medium or a psychic, and I guarantee that you too can do it. Find a quiet room, dim the lights and light a candle. Look at some photos of the person you wish to be with. If you have no pictures then hold an object that belonged to them. In short, try to concentrate and remember as many wonderful things as possible about that person. Let those memories now soar through your waking thoughts and inhabit your sleeping dreams. And that is the secret – the best final resting place you can find to bury a loved one is in your heart. This ground can never be disturbed, nor can the flowers placed there ever fade. In your heart the memories you cherish will be with you whenever you want and wherever you are. No matter where your loved ones are physically buried, their spirit will come to you if you need them. Whoever now dwells on the other side can be kept eternally alive through the power of your memories.

## Death is the biggest life experience of all

It is too easy to be paralysed by regret. It is much harder to accept the fact that we loved someone and in return were loved by them. We must remember the past, but not let it bring our futures to a sudden halt. The death of someone you love obviously provokes all sorts of different emotions and disturbs your body and soul in ways that nothing else will. This emotional energy is not bad and must not be swept under the carpet in the hope that it will just go away. Instead it must be used positively to try and carry on and live your own life as meaningfully as possible.

In order to manage life more successfully, we have to learn from our past experiences and how we reacted to them. Death may be the most painful experience of all, but it is important to focus on the learning rather than the pain. To do this we need to ask, 'What has this taught me? What lessons can I learn: about myself, about others and about my life? How can I use this new knowledge to change my thinking and behaviour and improve the quality of my life and that of others around me? Seeing things in this light, it is possible that death can have a positive and life-enhancing value. The readings that I give and the stories that I hear from people's everyday lives convince me that we should never give up. Life is always worth living – no matter how much despair you are in, there is much to look forward to.

## Learning to find life after a death

- We have a responsibility to go on living after our loved ones have passed on. Not only that but we should use their death to live our lives in a more fulfilling way.

- You will naturally feel negative but you must try to use your powers of positive thinking. *You are what you think.* Going forward, you can decide how you want to feel about a person's death. It can ultimately become a positive experience.

- Those in the spirit world are physically and mentally well. Even if they have died a violent or tragic death, they are reconciled and so should you be. They will always be in your heart, if you want them to be.

- Your loved ones do not want you to be dead to the world, they would rather see you honour their lives by carrying on with your life. If you don't, then it's you who have died, not them.

- Guilt is not a sign that you are grieving but simply a reluctance to move on. What's done is done. If you feel guilty about what happened between you and someone who has passed on, use the experience to make sure it doesn't happen again.

- The death of somebody gives us an opportunity to change our lives for the better. After the sadness, we need to embrace the light and use that emotional energy to learn from past experiences.

# 9.

# Life is for living

*'Life is something that everyone should
try at least once.'*

HENRY J TILLMAN

Here we are at the business end of the book. By now I'm hoping
that you are so full of the possibilities of life that you won't even
bother to read on! What I've talked about in this book is not a
result of any revolutionary thought on my part. It's not particularly new and it isn't terribly complicated. It's about realising
that life is for living and that no matter how much it throws at
us, no matter how much we may despair, we have a responsibility to live our lives in the most positive way possible. Listening
to the messages from our spirit contacts can provide us with lessons for the future, but it should not leave us stuck in the past.

I don't think you can be happy as a person, let alone as a
medium, unless you have known unhappiness. I feel I've been
through that and I've come out the other side. Today, after

several years of wondering where I fit in, I can say that I am beginning to find my balance in life. A large part of my life has been about discovering myself, discovering my mediumship, and discovering that my purpose in life is to be a link between the seen and the unseen worlds. I am in the fortunate position of knowing there is something more, that beyond this life our spirits do continue. However, I also believe we have a responsibility to the people that we love and care for who have passed over that we carry on living, because if not then we too are dead to the world.

I hope that some of the ideas in this book will have helped you think about the value and meaning of your life. I cannot claim to have it all worked out. I've made loads of mistakes and I face just as many challenges as the next person. Even as I write this there are new challenges being thrown at me. Will there be further tabloid backlashes against mediums? Will the public still be interested in what we have to offer? And most importantly, will I react in the most positive way, whatever the answers to these questions?

Many people go through life not wanting to be told the truth. Instead they want to receive validation, be told that what they are doing is right. However, in order to open ourselves up to change and to the potential of our lives, we need to admit that some of the things we have thought up till now may be preventing us from moving forward. Remember what I said in chapter 2: you are what you think. I believe we are all capable of changing our attitude to life and yes, to death if we want to. Events may be out of our control, but the way we allow them to affect us is not. Notice I said 'allow them'. That is deliberate because true life before death is about leading a life, not waiting for it to happen.

How often do you hear the phrase 'seize the day' and think, 'Yes, I should do that', but never really follow it up? How often do you think of calling your ageing mother or father but decide to put it off instead of doing it that moment? How long have you thought about changing jobs but done nothing about it? How many times has your son or daughter asked you to take them to see a film but you keep putting it off? Now, these may seem like relatively small, everyday occurrences and therefore not momentous enough to make a difference to our lives, but it's the little things we do, or don't do, that add up. If you think that you must wait for a watershed moment before you seize the day then you are mistaken. Our lives are made up of incremental moments that form the rich pattern that is each individual life. Life is also made up of minutes that pass all too quickly into hours, days then years. Blink and you'll miss it. Whatever your circumstances and whatever your age, you can still make a decision to change any aspect of your life that you are dissatisfied or unhappy with.

The suggestions and ideas I've given you come from what I've learned from in my communications with spirits as well as my interactions with their loved ones. It has been a privilege to be present when people start to see things in a different light; when they realise that they have only lost the physical person from their lives and they still have much to live for. It's exciting to watch them leave my house or the studio with a spring in their step, free of the burden they arrived with. As I said at the beginning, my ability as a medium is a gift but I am as normal as the next guy. With that in mind, I hope you will accept the following as a reminder that we are all learning together. I hope that in some small way I can help you live this precious life to the full until such time as you too pass to the other side.

## 15 steps to life before death

- Enjoy each moment for what it is, no matter how small. Even if you believe in reincarnation, you have only this life as you. 'Now' is a wonderful gift. Don't waste it dwelling on the past.
- The buck stops with you. You are responsible for everything that happens in your life. Even if you have not directly caused or created it, you can choose how to deal with it going forward. Remember you are not a victim; you are only a victim if you choose to be one. You are a person with choices.
- Remember, you are what you think. Choose to be happy. You cannot choose what happens to you but you can choose how to react to it. Try to look on the bright side of life and project a positive attitude. In this way you will encourage good things to come to you. People will be attracted to you and that in turn will increase your confidence.
- Don't think of negative occurrences as something abnormal. Incorporate them into your life as you would incorporate the positive, and then you will find they do not take over your life. Try to spend less time with negative people.
- Your destiny is not bound up in your background or family experience. You can choose what you become. If you are in a situation where a relationship has turned particularly sour and you are being hurt or abused by someone, it may be best to end or change the relationship.

- It is wrong to think that we can become great fonts of unlimited love for some family members; we are often just too different and may have to keep our relationship with them simply cordial and caring rather than deep and intimate.

- The ability to make friends is often based on a person's ability to tolerate differences rather than look for things in common. It is these differences that increase our appreciation of each other and the world. Look at your wider community as a source of contact and friendships.

- No matter what you feel someone has done to you, you must learn to let go. Don't let your life be destroyed by bitterness and anger.

- Forgiving someone does not mean absolving them of their responsibility. It means letting go of the pain and hurt you feel in your heart and reclaiming control over your life. You should not forgive as a gift to the person who has wronged you; instead do it as a gift to yourself.

- Spirituality is our attempt to make some sense of the world around us. Spirituality can have many definitions and many forms but in the end it is fundamentally about a search for inner peace, happiness, contentment and hope.

- By not talking about death we may lose our chance to make the most of the time we have with someone who is dying. It will be difficult but it will mean that when they do die we will have done our best.

- It is important to grieve for the loss. We are putting off that process if we keep asking, 'Why?' Instead we need to accept that death has happened and attempt to incorporate the event into our lives.
- Use the death of a loved one to affirm life. Learn from the experience and try to see death as a source of further inspiration for your life.
- Those in the spirit world are physically and mentally well. Even if they have died a violent or tragic death, they are reconciled and so should you be. They will always be in your heart, if you want them to be.
- Your loved ones do not want you to be dead to the world, they would rather see you honour their lives by carrying on with your life. If you don't, then it's you who have died, not them.

# Useful contact numbers

*This listing does not mean that the organisations mentioned below have reviewed or approved the contents of this book.*

## The Official Colin Fry Website
www.colinfry.com
To book theatre tickets, find out the latest news about Colin and purchase other Colin Fry merchandise.

## International Programme Marketing
Tel. 0207 515 5100
www.ipmtv.com
The company that makes *6ixth Sense* and Colin's other television programmes and that organises many of Colin's public appearances.

## Counselling Services

*Bereavement counselling*
UK:
### Compassionate Friends
www.compassionatefriends.co.uk
Bereavement support.
### Cruse Bereavement Care
Tel. 0870 167 1677
www.crusebereavementcare.org.uk
Exists to promote the wellbeing of bereaved people.

Australia and New Zealand:
**Caritas**
Tel. (02) 8382 9594
**NALAG** (Association of Loss and Grief)
Tel. (02) 9988 3376

*Counselling for those in despair*
UK:
**The Samaritans**
Tel: 08457 90 90 90
www.samaritans.org
Confidential emotional support for those experiencing
feelings of distress or despair, which may lead to suicide.

Australia and New Zealand:
**Living is For Everyone**
www.livingisforeveryone.com.au
Lists organisations who may help in time of crisis.

*Cancer support*
UK:
**Macmillan Cancer Support**
Tel. 0808 808 2020
www.macmillan.org.uk
Improves the lives of people affected by cancer.

Australia and New Zealand:
**Can-Survive (Aus)**
Tel. 1300 364673
www.can-survive.org
Offers a hopeline to those in need of support.

**Cancer Society of New Zealand Inc**
www.cancernz.org.nz
Offers contact details and support.

*Alcohol and Substance abuse counselling*
UK:
**Frank**
Tel. 0800 77 66 00
www.talktofrank.com
Information on drugs and guidance for those worried about
possible drug abuse.
**National Alcohol Helpline**
Tel. 0800 917 8282
http://www.patient.co.uk/showdoc/26738981/

Australia and New Zealand:
**Alcohol Drug Association** (NZ)
Tel. 0800 787 797
www.adanz.org.nz
**Narconon ANZD**
www.narconon.org
The Australian division of the international organisation
Narconon.

*AIDs and HIV counselling*
UK:
**The Terence Higgins Trust**
Tel. 0845 12 21 200
http://www.tht.org.uk/
Charity in the forefront of the fight against HIV and AIDs.

Australia and New Zealand:

**AIDS Action Council**

www.aidsaction.org.au

**Body Positive Inc, New Zealand**

www.bodypositive.org.nz

Website for those affected by AIDs or HIV.

*Domestic violence and rape counselling*

UK:

**National Domestic Violence Helpline**

Tel. 0808 2000 247

www.womensaid.org.uk

For suffers of domestic violence.

Australia and New Zealand:

**Domestic Violence Helpline**

Tel. 1800 656463

*Gay / Lesbian counselling*

UK:

**Lesbian & Gay Switchboard**

Tel. 0207 837 7324

www.queery.org.uk

Australia and New Zealand:

**Gay & Lesbian Switchboard**

Tel. (03) 9510 5488

www.vicnet.net.au

## Spiritualism & Mediumship Contacts

UK:

**Psychic Directory**

www.psychicdirectory.co.uk

Website lists psychic development contacts and spiritualists.

**United Spiritualists**

www.unitedspiritualists.org

Religious body supports the work of affiliated mediums and healers.

Australia and New Zealand:

**Spiritualism**

Home.vicnet.au

Lists contacts for Spiritualist churches in Australia and New Zealand.

## Making A Will

I believe that every responsible person should make a will. For information that is tailored to you personally, contact your local solicitor.

UK:

Citizens Advice Bureau

www.adviceguide.org.uk

Includes advice on making a will.

Australia and New Zealand:

**Webwombat**

www.webwombat.com.au

Search engine that will link you to a variety of websites that discuss wills etc.